GOVERNORS STATE UNIVERSITY
LIBRARY

DEMCO

Discipline, Achievement, and Race

Is Zero Tolerance the Answer?

Augustina H. Reyes

Rowman & Littlefield Education
Lanham, Maryland • Toronto • Oxford
2006

Published in the United States of America
by Rowman & Littlefield Education
A Division of Rowman & Littlefield Publishers, Inc.
A wholly owned subsidiary of The Rowman & Littlefield Publishing Group, Inc.
4501 Forbes Boulevard, Suite 200, Lanham, Maryland 20706
www.rowmaneducation.com

PO Box 317
Oxford
OX2 9RU, UK

British Library Cataloguing in Publication Information Available

Library of Congress Cataloging-in-Publication Data

Reyes, Augustina H., 1945–
    Discipline, achievement, and race : is zero tolerance the answer? / Augustina
H. Reyes.
        p.   cm.
    Includes bibliographical references.
    ISBN-13: 978-1-57886-450-8 (hardcover : alk. paper)
    ISBN-10: 1-57886-450-X (hardcover : alk. paper)
    ISBN-13: 978-1-57886-451-5 (pbk. : alk. paper)
    ISBN-10: 1-57886-451-8 (pbk. : alk. paper)
    1. School discipline—United States.   2. Minorities—Education—United States.
3. Academic achievement—United States.   I. Title.
LB3012.2.R49   2006
371.5—dc22   2005034532

∞ ™ The paper used in this publication meets the minimum requirements of
American National Standard for Information Sciences—Permanence of Paper for
Printed Library Materials, ANSI/NISO Z39.48-1992. Manufactured in the United
States of America.

Contents

Acknowledgments

My interest in zero tolerance discipline policies began during the final days of my tenure as a school trustee for the Houston Independent School District. In the late 1980s the school administration briefed the board on new policies that were going to affect school discipline reporting practices. The Texas Juvenile Commission was developing legislation that would affect Texas public schools. The first major change was that in the future the school district would report to the county juvenile authorities the names of all students who were removed from school for discipline infractions. Historically, school discipline was a responsibility for school principals or their designees, usually the assistant principal. The phrase "butts, buses, and books" is a historical depiction of the discipline responsibilities reserved for assistant principals. This was the first sign of a relationship between public schools and the body responsible for county juvenile crime. In 1995 the Texas Legislature developed and approved *Chapter 37 Law and Order* policy for school discipline. The policy formalized the relationship between public schools and county juvenile crime agencies.

Texas zero tolerance policy has grown from removal for major violations such as having drugs, guns, knives, and other weapons to class C misdemeanors for classroom disruptions. Class C misdemeanors require that a student go to court and defend the violation. While these experiences describe Texas conditions, zero tolerance policies are replicated throughout the United States. Texas is not unique. Research shows that zero tolerance is a national interest. While zero tolerance may appear as a discipline policy issue, it has expanded well beyond discipline. Zero tolerance affects social development, teacher preparation, and knowledge of classroom management, race biases, student achievement, and civil rights.

I would like to thank the many preservice principal preparation students from the University of Houston and Texas A&M University who have informed me about urban and rural school discipline practices to provide safe school environments while increasing student achievement and reducing the use of exclusionary zero tolerance policies.

I dedicate this book to my Mother, Jane Hernandez Reyes, who let it be known that while I lived in her house I had no First Amendment or Fourth Amendment rights. I thank Dr. Michael A. Olivas for his constant scholarly support and friendship. Finally, I thank Monsignor Jerome J. Martinez y Alire, rector of the Saint Francis Cathedral in Santa Fe, New Mexico, for constantly reminding me that my work is a gift.

1

Background and National Context: Criminalization of Student Behavior

Zero tolerance refers to the exclusionary, state-mandated school discipline policies that have gained national popularity for their "get tough" approach on student misconduct. Zero tolerance discipline policies became popular on the stage in Columbine, Colorado, and other states experiencing student killings. In 1974, an eighteen-year-old honor student shot and killed a janitor and firefighters in a well-planned attack on his school. On February 2, 1996, two students and one teacher were killed when a fourteen-year-old student started shooting during an algebra class in Moses, Washington. In 1997, one principal and one student were killed by a sixteen-year-old in Bethel, Alaska. The same year, two students were killed and seven were wounded by a student in Pearl, Mississippi—the student, who worshiped Satan, was considered an outcast. In December 1997, a fourteen-year-old killed three students and wounded five as they participated in student prayer in West Paducah, Kentucky. With the exception of student shootings in Baltimore, Maryland, and Richmond, Virginia, many of the student killings have occurred in rural or suburban communities. A national response to school shootings and the need for safe school environments resulted in the development of zero tolerance school discipline policies.

Since 1974 there have been thirty-seven school shootings. Following Columbine, school districts made enormous investments in school security equipment, including metal detectors, cameras, and student and staff identification card systems. Schools have limited the number of entrances to campuses and searched backpacks and lockers. Some schools have used bomb-sniffing dogs. Lock-down drills, hotlines, and campus police are used in

1

many campuses. Research on school shootings show that equipment alone will not keep guns and violent crimes out of the school. In 2000, a Palm Beach County, Florida, school student walked into a school and killed a teacher. The school was fully equipped with the most sophisticated security equipment, including a card-access system and a full-time guard. Principals have learned that expensive equipment is not enough to maintain a safe school environment.

The evidence from Columbine and successful campus crime-prevention efforts show that school climate and good relationships with students are the best crime prevention tools. According to a U.S. Secret Service report, in 75 percent of the school shootings, the students told someone else about the shootings (U.S. Secret Service, 2000). School districts in Twentynine Palms, California; Fort Collins, Colorado; Elmira, New York, have all prevented major violent crimes by using information provided by students and staff. Crime prevention comes from investments in resource personnel, counselors, staff development, and student development. Other resources include providing teachers and other staff with communication and management skills. The intent of zero tolerance policies that prevent violent crime is important for every school. While Department of Education reports show schools to be one of the safest places for our children, school safety should be the primary concern of every school principal (Snyder and Hoffman, 2000). School safety takes precedence over school testing and many other school programs. It is important that every school have a school crisis plan that focuses on school safety. Schools must be safe and secure for students, teachers, and staff members. Without a safe and secure school, teaching and learning cannot take place.

The concerns with zero tolerance policies are the thoughtlessness with which they are implemented and the extension of crime-prevention policies to daily school behavior defined as discipline infractions. The lack of administrative flexibility and discretion led to student expulsions for the possession of Midol, a misplaced butter knife in a truck, and coming to school without a uniform when the family could not afford to buy the uniform. The original intent of providing school safety by keeping guns, other weapons, drugs, tobacco, and violence off the school campus has evolved to the criminalization of student behavior. The overrepresentation of Latino, African American, low-income, poor, and at-risk students in zero tolerance discipline categories fueled a debate about the real intent of these policies. Are these policies effective? Are zero tolerance policies equitable? Is the purpose of zero tolerance to reduce school violence or an elaborate public policy scheme to exclude low-income, special education, academically at-risk, and minority students from school? Are there more reasonable alternatives that also produce better achievement?

ZERO TOLERANCE: THE WAR AGAINST DRUGS

Zero tolerance policies are not a new phenomenon. They have been used by the federal government in the military and in the War Against Drugs (Katzenstein and Reppy, 1999). In the military zero tolerance means that the institution will not tolerate those who do not follow the policies and guidelines governing the behavior of military personnel. It does not mean that there will be zero incidents of these infractions (Katzenstein and Reppy, 1999). It does not mean that sexual harassment, discrimination, spousal abuse, and drug problems in the military will be eliminated. They will just be decreased. In order for zero tolerance to work in the military, the fundamental reorientation of military cultures was required (Katzenstein and Reppy, 1999). The military used a zero tolerance policy on drugs, and after twenty years of zero tolerance on drugs, in 2001 positive drug testing increased by 29 percent. The military saw improvements in reducing drug usage, but did not declare a victory for zero tolerance. In the 1980s zero tolerance became a policy in the War Against Drugs under U.S. Attorney General Edwin Meese. By 1990 the policy was abandoned without success. In 1994, the federal government adopted zero tolerance policies for weapons, drugs, and violence. Zero tolerance policies were picked up by public schools with the first sightings in Orange County, California, and Louisville, Kentucky (Verdugo, 2005). The policy was first applied by Donald Batista, superintendent of the Yonkers school system in New York with many features that are present in today's zero tolerance policies (Verdugo, 2005).

THE DUTY AND RESPONSIBILITY OF TEACHERS AND PRINCIPALS FOR SCHOOL DISCIPLINE

Historically, school discipline has been the duty and the responsibility of school teachers and principals. Schools operate under the rules and regulations of the local board of education and the state. Nowhere is that more evident than in student discipline. School administrators and teachers have wide discretionary authority in disciplining students. Teacher discretionary authority and police power is derived from the legal doctrine of in loco parentis and several legal cases including *New Jersey v. TLO* (Rosenberg, 2003). According to the doctrine, the principal and the teacher stand in the place of the parent while the student is in school. Since the principal and the teacher stand in the place of the parent and the unique relationship between the parent and the child, educators have authority over matters that even the board of education may not have (McCarthy, Cambron-McCabe, and Thomas, 2004; Rosenberg, 2003). Courts have held that school officials stand in loco parentis and have the right to exercise supervision, the right to control students, the right to police power, and an obligation to protect them while students are entrusted to the school (Rosenberg, 2003). Teachers, administrators, and other school staff assume the role of parents with teachers as the frontline for student discipline.

The purpose of zero tolerance is to remove "disruptive" students from the classroom to create a learning environment where students who want to learn can learn and teachers can teach (Reyes, 2001). In theory it is difficult to quarrel with this premise, but as is the case in life and educational policy, the end result is not as efficacious as the theory. This system attempts to protect one group and identify another group as the predators and delinquent troublemakers who need to be suspended, expelled, or referred to a separate environment, including the criminal system. Weapons, drug abuse, and violence threaten the safety of students and teachers while disruptions undermine the learning process (Blumenson and Nilsen, 2003). The difficult question is whether or not zero tolerance after ten years of implementation is the most effective method to judge adolescent behavior.

PURPOSE OF THE BOOK

Student behavior and discipline have historically been the responsibilities of school administrators and teachers. According to Tyack (1974), some early school masters had to be able to fight off the school bully. In a more modern period, student behavior and discipline are governed by school district rules and regulations. Student behavior assumes that there is this body of knowledge embodied in behavioral theory, student development theory, and classroom management theory and skills. Teachers and administrators acquire this knowledge base in preservice and staff development activities. The student behavioral, developmental, and discipline knowledge and skills form the repertoire for classroom management and behavior. Historically, student discipline was the responsibility of school administrators and classroom teachers.

In the 1990s, the context of education in the United States was changing. Accountability became a way to measure school productivity. The image of public schools was constantly under fire from the media. New school organizational models grounded in public choice became policy realities. Public school clients and their behavior became a focus of the media. In 1999, several school shootings and Columbine, Colorado, happened. School violence and public perceptions of school violence became a risk that no school district or school administrator wanted to take. The question for every school principal in the United States became, "How do we identify early warning signs of students who might be prone to violence?" Every threat of violence or harm to others is serious. State legislatures all over the United States enacted zero tolerance school discipline policies modeled after the Public Law 103-227 of the 1994 Gun-Free Schools Act.

Zero tolerance policies were elaborately intertwined with state, county, and juvenile and law enforcement departments. Gradually, state policies removed the responsibility for student behavior and student discipline from the hands of school administrators and teachers to the forces of criminal law and external law enforcement agents. Zero tolerance policy proposes to treat all threats equally, resulting in increased removal of students from the regular classroom into suspension, expulsion, on-campus alternative education programs, and off-campus alternative education program. Zero tolerance policy took great efforts to identify discretionary and mandatory offenses and on-campus and off-campus offenses.

George Will (2000) described zero tolerance as a new wave of "bureaucratic legalism" over what has been viewed as norm behavior. According to Will (2000), civilized life depends on informal rules and measures or the social wink that prevents mundane conflicts from becoming legal extravaganzas or opportunities for moral exhibitions. He defines the new student discipline ethos as having "profoundly changed what was once deemed usual, if annoying behavior by adolescents. No longer is the playground scrap or the kickball tussle deemed a right of passage best settled by a teacher who orders the combatants to their corners, hears out the two sides and demands apologies and a handshake" (A3). Zero tolerance has evolved from the intent of controlling guns and crime in the schools to an all-purpose solution for any discipline misbehavior regardless of seriousness.

The purpose of this book is to increase the school principal's understanding of zero tolerance policies and their lifelong consequences. Research shows that school leaders and improved school organizations—management, governance, culture, and climate—can more effectively reduce student disruptions (Gottfredson, 1986). What are zero tolerance policies, and how do they contribute to increased illiteracy, dropping out of school, and the creation of a school-to-prison pipeline for a disproportionately high number of students of color? How does zero tolerance reinforce deficit thinking in American schools? This book will identify and discuss the policy and the practices of zero tolerance nationally and for selected states.

Disciplinary Alternative Education Programs (DAEP) and the expansion of zero tolerance into school disruptions will be analyzed. The professional beliefs of teachers and principals in context of a national and state school discipline policy environment that has silenced the professional beliefs of principals and teachers will be explored. What do they think will ensure a safe and productive learning environment and also guarantee an opportunity to learn? How do zero tolerance policies affect student achievement and staying in school?

THE NATIONAL CONTEXT

The 1997 case of Timothy Narvares was not unique to Texas. The stage for the Navares case was set during the 1990s when a number of school shootings became high profile news events, culminating with the April 1999 killings at Columbine High School. News coverage and expert testimony predicted a wave of juvenile crime, even as the U.S. Department of Justice (1999) reported a 20 percent decrease in crime and a 30 percent decrease in juvenile crime during 1990–1999 (U.S. Congressional Hearings before the Subcommittee on Select Education of the House Committee on Education and the Workforce, Juvenile Crime Control and Delinquency Prevention Act of 2001, 2001). During this period, U.S. Census data showed an increase of minority populations, particularly a growth bubble that represented minority youth (Gibson and Jung, 1990). Public testimony predicted a juvenile crime bomb with the "coming of 40 million 10 year old and under . . . fatherless, godless and jobless" (Butterfield, 1995, A18). John J. Dilulio predicted the "coming of superpredators" with the advent of tens of thousands of "severely morally impoverished juvenile super predators" (Dilulio, 1995, 23 in Blumenson & Nilsen, 2003). According to Dilulio, the superpredators "fear neither the stigma of arrest nor the pain of imprisonment. . . . They will do what comes naturally: murder, rape, rob, assault, burglarize, deal deadly drugs, and get high" (23).

School districts across the United States set out to develop school safety plans with which to attack the predicted waves of juvenile crime. School districts in collaboration with the offices of state juvenile justice officials, including juvenile judges, and other state policy makers, broke with the historical traditions in the way public schools dealt with student discipline. Districts across the United States developed "zero tolerance" policies that were codified in the state statutes of education and in criminal procedures. The zero tolerance policies gave absolute power to juvenile authorities in collaboration with school officials. The goal of the new policy was to remove students who were troublemakers from the classroom through suspension or expulsion. The new collaboration required that if a student commits an illegal offense off school grounds, juvenile authorities are to report back to the school districts that must remove the student from school, as they did with Timothy Navares (Texas Code of Criminal Procedure, Article 15.27[a]). Forty-one states require that if the school removes a student from school for any of the criminal offenses outlined in the state zero tolerance policy, the district is required to report the incident to the juvenile authorities (Harvard, 2000). School discipline was no longer an issue of adolescent behavior; it became an issue of criminal record.

CHAPTER 2: DEFINING ZERO TOLERANCE

Zero tolerance refers to public school discipline policy that applies automatic, prescribed, mandatory sanctions for student discipline infractions with little or no consideration to the conditions, circumstances, intent, or understanding of the individual committing the offense (Blumenson and Nilsen, 2003). Zero tolerance policies are enforced by school officials who may not have or may choose not to exercise any discretion and flexibility. Zero tolerance policies mandate expulsion and suspension for specific discipline infractions that historically were dealt with using counseling, mediation, teacher intervention, or teacher classroom management techniques. The policy only considers whether or not the student committed the specified offense. For example, a butter knife was found in the back of the truck belonging to an honor student who denied knowing how it got there. The superintendent had no reason to suspect that the student was lying; however, under the law, that was not his decision. The state policy compelled him to expel the student.

Zero tolerance policies were incorporated into a national crime prevention effort with three major categories. The first category was the development of violence prevention and conflict resolution programs in school. For example, the Texas legislature mandated that all public school teachers receive training in mediation and conflict management. The Safe Schools Act of 1994 (PL 103-227) and the Safe and Drug-Free Schools and Communities Act of 1994 (PL 103-382) provided funding for peer mediation, conflict resolution, and other violence prevention programs (Casella, 2003). The second category attempted to mandate gun control laws. The Gun-Free School Zones Act of 1990 (PL 101-647) prohibits firearms within 1,000 feet of school property. The final federal crime prevention effort focused on punitive and judicial forms of school discipline. The Gun-Free Schools Act (PL 103-227) mandated that schools expel students for a minimum of one year for bringing a gun to school. The federal laws were tied to federal funding for public schools through the Elementary and Secondary Education Act (ESEA) of 1965. The ESEA required that federal funding be withheld from school districts that did not enforce the PL 103-227.

While the federal law provides a provision to modify an expulsion based on extraordinary or mitigating circumstances, states have adopted more prescriptive policies (Bowman, 2002). Since 1994, state zero tolerance policies have expanded from guns to weapons to drugs to classroom disruption (TEC, 37.124). Some have criticized the use of zero tolerance policies as an elaborate legal technique to get rid of kids who schools do not want (Bowman, 2002; Reyes, 2001).

Zero tolerance policies in Texas have three distinct sections. Since they are modeled after the Gun-Free Act of 1994, policies related to guns and other weapons serve as a foundation for state zero tolerance policies. The second major component of zero tolerance policies is a section that provides local districts with the discretion to develop, publish, and clearly display local district discipline policies or code of student behavior. The third component that has emerged from zero tolerance policies is a section that identifies class A, class B, and class C misdemeanors for school-related infractions. This section identifies behavioral infractions for which a student must be given a ticket by a peace officer and defend himself in one of three judicial jurisdictions (TEC §37.104, 2004). Class C misdemeanors represent the lowest level of criminal behavior and for defendants sixteen years of age and younger, an offense that "may" be expunged from their criminal record (C.C.P. Art. 55.01, 2005; C.C.P. Art. 45.055, 2005).

Zero Tolerance: Opportunities Suspended

Zero tolerance is contrary to the best educational practices. Zero tolerance policies set equal expectations on an already unequal playing field, reject developmental needs of children, deny educational opportunities by contributing to dropouts, produce poor achievement, and criminalize student behavior (Harvard, 2000). Hispanics in the United States complete school at the rate of 52 percent compared with a rate of 72 percent for Whites (ETS, 2005). Zero tolerance only accelerates the dropout rate.

Removal from school or from the regular classroom for suspension or expulsion reverses all the research and common knowledge about "time on task" (Berliner, 1988). School attendance laws are predicated on the belief that if a student is not in school, learning cannot take place (Achilles and Smith, 1999). Mandatory school attendance and keeping students in school have always been a national school policy (Alexander, 2001). The correlation between poor attendance, exclusions from school, and dropping out of school are only exacerbated by zero tolerance policies (Achilles and Smith, 1999; Gottfredson et al., 1993; Harvard, 2000; Irvine, 1991; Skiba and Peterson, 1999). According to the report of the Harvard Civil Rights Project (2000), there are indications that removal from the regular classroom will cause students to drop out of school. More than 30 percent of the sophomores who drop out of school have also been suspended. Students suspended in school are also more likely to be incarcerated, creating the school-to-prison pipeline (Harvard, 2000; Rumbaut, 2005).

In an effort to provide a separate, supervised educational placement for dangerous and disruptive students rather than a "three-day student expulsion, which is nothing more than an unsupervised street furlough for delinquent students to commit crimes," twenty-six states provide DAEPs (Harvard, 2000; Reyes, 2001). The DAEPs exclude students from the regular classroom, cause students to get behind in the regular curriculum, and increase school failure and dropping out of school.

Zero Tolerance: The Texas Case

In 1995, the 74th Texas Legislature enacted the Safe Schools Act, Chapter 37 of the Texas Education Code. The Texas Safe Schools Act did not use the phrase "zero tolerance"; however, it used the highly prescriptive, non-negotiable requirements of zero tolerance policy and officially removed teachers and administrators from the student discipline decision-making process. The school's responsibility for discipline became a role of complying with the law. The policy required that school districts' boards of trustees "shall . . . adopt a student code of conduct" (37.001). It used the language of "shall" for required student removal from the regular classroom and the language of "may" be removed in cases with administrator flexibility. It also listed specific infractions. "A teacher may remove from class a student who" repeatedly interferes with the teacher's ability to teach (37.002[b] [1]). "A student shall be removed from class and placed in a DAEP" for the offense of false alarms, felonies, assault, marijuana, drugs, alcohol, public lewdness, and other offenses (37.006). Other listings include cases for which a student "shall be expelled" (37.007).

State policy allows students to be removed from regular instructional classroom by several means. Students may be removed based on Chapter 37 policies or by local district policy as defined in the district student code of conduct (36.001). The role of school administrators is crucial to the administration of zero tolerance policies. The principal or other appropriate administrator, usually an assistant principal, must be responsible for all student removals from the regular instructional class. The state policy for student behavior provides five options for mandatory and discretionary removals out of the regular classroom. The options include removal to a DAEP, expulsions, out-of-school suspension, in-school suspension, and for urban areas, the Juvenile Justice Alternative Education Program (JJAEP).

Like many other states, the Texas legislature created the "Safe Schools Act" to comply with a federal mandate. Officially, the 1994 Gun-Free Schools Act provided the impetus for mandatory student expulsions and suspensions. It conditioned federal aid to the schools upon the state's adoption of policies to remove students who bring weapons to school. The policy required that students be removed from school for one year. It also mandated that state policy report these students to law enforcement authorities.

In practice, the policy of *Subchapter G, Safe Schools, Chapter 37, Discipline: Law and Order* targets urban, low-income, at-risk, and male student populations who are disproportionately minority. The 2000–2001 Texas PEIMS summary data for the state discipline program showed that of the 1,675,746 discipline actions recorded, approximately 95 percent were for discretionary reasons. Only 5 percent were for mandatory removal reasons. A total of 798,666 students were removed from the regular instruction classroom a total of 2.1 times per student. Zero tolerance policies served to criminalize the behavior of a disproportionate number of minority students.

CHAPTER 3: DISCIPLINARY ALTERNATIVE EDUCATION PROGRAMS

Reactions to school shootings and perceived school violence spurred state legislatures to develop safe school legislation to frame all student discipline actions and consequences. Theoretically, the most severe disciplinary infractions lead to student isolations or the use of DAEPs. In practice, DAEPs in the United States and Texas were used to isolate problem students. The disproportionate enrollment of urban, African American, Hispanic, low-income, at-risk, and male students raises concern about the intent and practice of DAEP policy. In 2004, African Americans made up 13.5 percent of all the first graders in Texas and 37 percent of all the first graders and 38 percent of all the third graders in the DAEP (Texas Education Agency, 2005). A common trend in zero tolerance violations is the disproportionate number of children of color who are disciplined or separated out of the regular school into disciplinary alternative education programs as early as the first grade.

In the Toledo, Ohio, schools, 65 percent of discipline violations were issued to minority students (Rimer, 2004). Concerns have been expressed that *Subtitle G, Safe Schools, Chapter 37, Discipline Law and Order* of the Texas

Education Code isolate some students for minor infractions creating an elaborate system to justify student segregation. This chapter defines DAEP and discusses the operation of Texas DAEPs in the context of state policy. It summarizes DAEP program enrollment, teacher certification, achievement, and curriculum policies. This chapter also defines and describes the JJAEP, discusses JJAEP policy, and discusses how JJAEPs are used.

Subtitle G, Safe Schools, Chapter 37 Discipline Law and Order was created to provide alternative education settings for behavioral management with disruptive students (Texas Education Code Annotated, 2001). Disruptive students or "students not able to function in the structure of the regular school setting" are to be removed from their regular classroom setting and placed in an alternative education setting based upon elaborate state and local discipline policies, rules, regulations, and procedures (Texas Education Agency, 2000–2001). DAEPs are intended for students who commit crimes (Texas Education Agency, 2002). DAEPs are funded using state compensatory education funds intended for low-income and at-risk students (Texas Education Code Annotated, 29.081[d] [6]). Students are removed from their regular classroom to suspension, expulsion, or alternative education (Texas Education Code Annotated, Chapter 37, 2001). Alternative education placements range from in-school detention/suspension centers to disciplinary alternative education programs (DAEP) primarily off-campus to juvenile justice alternative education programs (JJAEP).

Juvenile Justice Alternative Education Program

In 1995, Senate Bill I mandated that all counties with a population of 125,000 or more operate a JJAEP under the jurisdiction of the county juvenile board (37.011). JJAEP were exclusively mandated in urban areas for youth who are on probation or deferred prosecution (37.0011[b] [1] [2]). While a judge may place a student in the JJAEP, the largest number of JJAEP referrals come from DAEPs and other school district referrals for the discretionary violation of "serious and persistent misbehavior" (Texas Juvenile Probation Commission, 2001–2002) In 2000–2001, there were 6,832 entrances into Texas JJAEPs, of which 52 percent, or 3,537 adolescent entrances, were for persistent misbehavior in the DAEP. While no data were available on student academic ability, data did show that 55 percent to 70 percent of all DAEP placements were categorized as academically at risk. In 2004, 80 percent of all JJAEP placements were academically at risk. Fifty-two percent of the JJAEP students committed no crime, but they were put in the same facility as students who committed murder, felony drug offenses, weapons offenses, and other serious crimes. Rather than provide a systems approach to improve achievement, DAEPs were created to remove low testers. What the JJAEP does with the 1,593 students who committed serious crimes should be the intent of zero tolerance; however, in practice, the JJAEP as a facility can only survive financially by contracting with school districts to incarcerate the persistent misbehavior students, exposing them to real criminals and creating new entrances into the school-to-prison pipeline.

CHAPTER 4: THE COURTROOM DRAMA

Chapter 4 discusses the evolution of zero tolerance policies from policies intended to control criminal activity of guns, drugs, and felonies to policies intended to control student development. During a period of adolescent development when students need adults to guide the behavior of future citizens, instead of guidance they receive citations.

Zero tolerance was intended to remove students who engage in criminal conduct, including felonies; assaults or terrorist threats; using, providing, or possessing drugs; and public lewdness or indecent exposure, receive deferred prosecution for a felony (TEC 37.006; 37.007; 37.124). In ten years, the policy has evolved to one that criminalizes student development and the acts students commit as they mature in development. State policy defines some student misbehavior (class B or class C misdemeanors) as subjective acts of school disruption. The policy requires that students be formally charged and receive tickets from the school, municipal, county police, or some other peace officer. The student is entered into a criminal system database and must defend himself in one of three judicial jurisdictions (Rimer, 2004; TEC §37.104). In Ohio, Virginia, Kentucky, and Florida, juvenile court judges are complaining that their courts are being flooded with discipline cases that the school should be handling (Rimer, 2004).

A judge in Ohio thinks that the stringent laws of zero tolerance have gone too far. "We're demonizing children" (Rimer, 2004, A1). The same judge expressed a concern about the rise in school-related cases in the judicial system. Out of 1,727 cases, 2 percent, or 34 of the Ohio cases, were for serious incidents (Rimer, 2004). In this example of zero tolerance, there were 1,727 adolescents who were targeted and processed as criminals for 34 serious incidents. In a Texas case, a judge probed into a school attendance violation case when several teachers wrote letters to the judge attesting to what a good student the defendant was, pleading with the judge not to fine the student. Upon probing, the judge found that the student was not attending school because the family could not afford the uniform required by the school. Judges who sit and hear zero tolerance cases in the United States are concerned about overcrowded dockets created by student misbehavior cases. While as many as 2 percent are serious cases as in Ohio, many more are frivolous cases that require discipline management, special services, social services, health services, literacy development, mentoring, mediation, and cross-cultural or other social skills development. When a serious drug violation is given the same citation as a dress code violation, what is the real message that schools are sending to students? Rather than providing guidance by forming a community, parent, business, and school task force to get to the bottom of what is causing students to distribute over-the-counter drugs to school peers, the case is turned over to a judge. The same judge must hear seventy similar cases in three hours. If the message of care is important to students, that is not the message they are getting from a system that gives them a ticket and turns the issue over to the local judge.

As class C misdemeanor student misconduct cases fill judicial dockets, the nature of zero tolerance becomes more public. Public courtroom observations produce mostly questionable cases that reinforce concerns about the disruption of education for many students. In one courtroom observation, it was noted that most of the students and their parents were Spanish speakers. In 80 percent of the cases students were nonliterate. When asked how he concluded that they were nonliterate, he replied, "When I ask them to sign their sentencing papers, they can't read where to sign" (Fraga, 2004).

In another courtroom, Judge Johanna was observed attempting to provide counseling from the bench for all seventy of the class C misdemeanor defendants that she must clear between 1 p.m. and 5 p.m. As the courtroom curtain opens, one is reminded of all the rehearsals that brought the cast to court on this Friday afternoon. Each defendant was given a ticket by a peace officer in the schools for conduct as identified in the state zero tolerance policy. Offenses include trespassing on school property after class hours, disruptive activities, disruption of classes, disruption of transportation, and disorderly conduct or fighting. Any of these offenses could be very dangerous, but subjective interpretations may also create a parent's worst nightmare. School personnel charge the student with the crime. The student is referred to the school assistant principal and a peace officer writes the ticket. The ticket is filed with a municipal judge, a county judge, or the state juvenile court depending on the state judicial rules. Each student formally enters the criminal justice system when the ticket and the student are assigned a database identification number in the Justice Information Management System (JIMS). The student is formally notified of the charges and given a court date. All students must be accompanied by a parent or guardian. The stage is set for court hearings.

The chief constable announces "All rise" as Judge Johanna enters. The Judge announces, "Under Procedural Code 45.055, once a student turns eigh-

teen years old 'they' may petition the court to have their case expunged"
(Delgado, 2004). The cast representing the state include the judge, a district
attorney, and a social worker. The cast representing the students include a
command performance by at least one parent and an attorney for the more
advantaged student. The judge announces, "For many of you this is your first
time in a courtroom and I hope your last."

The drama of poverty, social interactions, language, literacy, race, and
serious misbehavior issues will be played out one afternoon in seventy mini-
dramas. The majority of the students are minorities and males. The most serious cases will be for "disorderly conduct, fighting," and making threats.
Misdemeanor drug offenses will also be heard. One case, more about being
poor than discipline, involved a teen who fell asleep in class. When the
teacher asked another student to wake the student, a fight broke out. The student was properly ticketed and sent to court. In the court room, the parent
explained to the judge that she was disabled and fighting migraine headaches.
Both she and her husband were hospitalized. She requested an extension on
paying court fees because she did not have the money to pay the forty-eight
dollars. The judge referred the student for testing, which was scheduled
through the social worker provided by the county. Another case was a mod-
ern-day Internet prank between two high school girls. Someone posted a pim-
ple story about another student on the Internet. The affected student assumed
her rival posted the story and confronted the student in the school hallway. A
fight broke out and both students were ticketed. Disruption of transportation
cases included one case for a student jumping out of the bus using the emergency exit. In every case, Judge Johanna counsels students saying, "If someone walks up to you in a threatening way, you need to pull away to avoid a
fight." In most cases, she will recommend anger management classes or some
other behavior management techniques and deferred adjudication.

The names of all the students who commit class C misdemeanor offenses
of zero tolerance policies will be entered into a criminal justice information
management system. While their criminal records are expungable offenses
upon the age of majority, 25 percent of Judge Johanna's cases will not return
to expunge their teen record (citation). The court experience will affect students differently. The few students who walk into court with an attorney will
have the advantage of proper legal representation; however, that is only one
of the seventy cases. It is the student who walks into the courtroom and
announces that they have transferred from their home school to another
school that is most at risk of dropping out of school. By transferring out of
the school that issued the ticket, they are removed from the campus accountability records (TEA, 2004). While state accountability rules require all students to be tested, test scores for students who transfer cannot be attributed

to any particular campus; they can only be included in the district scores (TEA, 2004).

In-school suspensions in Texas increased 20 percent from 1998–1999 to 2003–2004. Out-of-school suspensions in Texas increased by 28 percent during the same period. Murder decreased from eleven cases in 1998–1999 to less than five cases in 2003–2004, or a decrease of over 50 percent. Firearm violations decreased from 542 in 1998–1999 to 176 in 2003–2004, or 68 percent. While not even one murder or one gun should be allowed in a school, zero tolerance appears to work in decreasing serious crime. Increases in out-of-school and in-school suspensions indicate that for lesser behavioral-based suspension violations, zero tolerance is not working. Increasing the stakes by ticketing students and introducing the criminal system into student behavioral management will only serve to deny many students an opportunity to an education.

CHAPTER 5: A BATTLE EACH DAY; TEACHERS TALK ABOUT DISCIPLINE, SUSPENSIONS, AND ZERO TOLERANCE POLICY

During an era of demanding school accountability and zero tolerance policies, the teacher's authority to maintain student discipline in the classroom has been compromised. Teachers are constantly under pressure to teach a curriculum that will increase the school's accountability rating. The priority for teachers in states with accountability testing is to prepare students for testing. Often, teachers must decide what they will not do, including reducing parent contact and classroom behavior management.

As the debate on the fairness and effectiveness of zero tolerance in the United States has evolved, the voices of teachers have been quietly silenced. The role of teachers in school discipline has evolved from one of authority and responsibility for classroom discipline to one of obeying and implementing state law. Yet, regardless of state policy, teachers remain the frontline keeper of student discipline. It is the teacher who must decide whether or not to initiate classroom disruption or other discipline referrals or to manage classroom discipline in the classroom. While some teacher organizations use zero tolerance as a technique to organize teachers and increase membership, others oppose zero tolerance. Most teachers feel the need to have options for removing students from the classroom. Some teachers feel that disruptive students take precious time from instructional time for those who want to learn. They do not have time for student behavioral management. They need all their time to prepare students for accountability testing. There are also those teachers who actually subvert zero tolerance policies so as to spare students what they perceive as overly harsh punishments. Since teacher voices have been silenced in this debate, there is no research on how teachers make decisions about zero tolerance policies.

The purpose of this chapter is to report the findings identified after conducting five focus groups of public school teachers in middle and high schools in one New England state. Through these focus groups, we sought to better understand what drives teachers' attitudes toward the use of zero tolerance and other exclusionary disciplinary measures in their schools, and whether these are related to the types of schools they teach in, the level of support they feel from their administration, their level of experience, and the population of students they teach.

CHAPTER 6: EXCLUSION IS NOT THE ONLY ALTERNATIVE: THE CHILDREN LEFT BEHIND PROJECT

Nationally, local school districts operate under the governance of local boards of education and the rules of the state legislature. Historically, school administrators and teachers have had wide discretionary authority in student discipline. Teacher discretionary authority in school discipline is derived from the legal doctrine of in loco parentis. According to the doctrine, the principal and the teacher stand in the place of the parent while the student is in school. Since the principal and the teacher stand in the place of the parent and the unique relationship between the parent and the child, they have authority over matters that even the board of education may not have. Courts have held that school officials stand in loco parentis and have the right to exercise supervision and control over students as well as an obligation to protect them while students are entrusted to the school (Alexander and Alexander, 1998). Teachers, administrators, and other school staff assume the role of parents for students in their care.

In the 1960s and 1970s, there were several major student cases affirming student constitutional rights, including due process rights under the Fourteenth Amendment and protection of Fourth Amendment rights to unreasonable searches (*New Jersey v. T.L.O.*, 1985; *Goss v. Lopez*, 1975). While the cases of the 1960s and 1970s defined student constitutional rights, they also reaffirmed the duty of teachers and principals to maintain discipline in the schools (McCarthy, Cambron-McCabe, and Thomas, 2004). Contrary to historical practices, state-imposed zero tolerance policies have reduced the historical discretion and flexibility that school officials held in school discipline. In many cases, principals and teachers have been silenced.

In this chapter, Karega Rausch and Russell Skiba will focus on the context of a national and state school discipline policy environment that has silenced the professional beliefs of principals and teachers. A growing research base suggests that the philosophy and approach to zero tolerance has failed as an intervention to advance student learning, improve school climate, and provide equitable results or to ensure school safety. Yet, it remains the preferred school discipline management approach of most school administrators. The fear of being the next Columbine principal, a perception of inadequate alternative resources, a belief that the only way to keep schools safe and productive is to remove students who threaten the learning environment, and policy mandates hinder the implementation of alternative discipline management approaches.

The current popularity of zero tolerance, however, does not mean that all educational leaders ascribe to this paradigm. In fact, there are many school principals who explicitly do not believe in the tenets of zero tolerance and actively promote alternative activities to ensure a safe and productive learning environment without removing students from the opportunity to learn. Moreover, emerging evidence suggests frequent use of student removal from the learning context may have deleterious academic consequences that are especially noteworthy in an era of academic accountability. This chapter will describe many of the philosophies and approaches of principals interviewed as part of the Children Left Behind project at the University of Indiana, an endeavor seeking to begin a statewide dialogue about disciplinary philosophy, policy, and practice, and disseminate research-validated and locally generated alternative disciplinary practices to key educational stakeholders in an attempt to influence disciplinary practice and policy in one midwestern state.

CHAPTER 7: CONCLUSIONS

Current research and the interviews in this book describe numerous successful alternative student discipline strategies that result in increased student achievement. There is a need to analyze zero tolerance data, reevaluate zero tolerance policies, refocus on the original intent of zero tolerance, and provide teachers and administrators with the time and resources to develop tomorrow's citizens. Mentoring, anger management, peer mediation, cross-cultural understanding, and the use of behavior models like Consistency Management all require time from the school day and funding for staff development and materials. Zero tolerance was never intended to segregate minority, low-income, and at-risk students. It was intended to remove drugs, guns, other weapons, murders, and students recommended by the courts. It was not intended to remove students who disrupt the classroom. Classroom management and other techniques were intended to control classroom behavior. Innovative alternative schools were intended for nonliterate students who misbehave when they do not understand the instruction. Teachers and administrators have the capability to restore discipline in the classroom but must have the time and resources to complete the mission.

REFERENCES

Achilles, C. M., and Smith, P. S. (1999). Stimulating the academic performance of pupils. In L. Hughes (ed.), *The Principal* (pp. 213–248). Upper Saddle River, NJ: Prentice-Hall.

Alexander, K., and Alexander, D. M. (1998). *American Public School Law*. Belmont, CA: West/Wadsworth.

Alexander, K., and Alexander, D. M. (2001). *American Public School Law*. Fourth edition. Belmont, CA: West/Wadsworth.

Berliner, D. (1988). Simple views of effective teaching and a simple theory of classroom instruction. In D. D. Berliner and B. Rosenshine (eds.), *Talks to Teachers* (pp. 93–110). New York: Random House.

Blumenson, E., and Nilsen, E. (2003). One strike and you're out? Constitutional constraints on zero tolerance in public education. *Washington University Law Quarterly 81*(1), 65–117.

Bowman, D. H. (2002, April 10). Interpretations of zero tolerance vary. *Education Week*, p. 30.

Butterfield, F. (1995, November 19). Crime continues to decline, but experts warn of coming "storm" of juvenile violence. *The New York Times*, pp. A18.

Casella, R. (2003). Zero tolerance policies in schools: Rationale, consequences, and alternatives. *Teachers College Record 105*(5), 872–892.

Delgado, J. (2004). Interview with J. Delgado conducted December 4, 2004.

Delgado, J. (2004). Observations of public proceedings in Harris County Justice of the Peace Court on December 3, 2004.

Dilulio, J. (1995, November 27). The coming of the super-predators. In E. Blumenson and E. Nilsen, One strike and you're out? *Washington University Law Quarterly 81*(1), 65–117.

Educational Testing Service. (2005). *One-Third of the Nation: Rising Dropout Rates and Declining Opportunities*. Princeton, NJ: ETS.

Fraga, D. (2004). Observations of public judicial proceedings in City of Houston Municipal Teen Court on November 22, 2004.

Gibson, C., and Jung, K. (1990). Population division: Historical census statistics on population total by race,1790 to 1990, and by Hispanic origin, 1970 to 1990, for the United States regions, divisions, and states. (U.S. Census Bureau Report No. 56). Retrieved

May 24, 2004, from www.census.gov/population/documentation/twps0056/twps0056 .pdf.

Goss v. Lopez, 419 U.S, 565 (1975).

Gottfredson, D. (1986). Promising strategies for improving student behavior. Paper presented on Student Discipline strategies of the Office of Educational Research and Improvement. U.S. Department of Education, Washington, D.C.

Gottfredson, D., Gottfredson, G. D., and Hybl, L. G. (1993). Managing adolescent behavior: A multi-year, multi-school study. *American Educational Research Journal 30*(1), 179–215.

Harvard University Advancement Projects and Civil Rights Project. (2000). Opportunities suspended: The devastating consequences of zero tolerance and school discipline. Retrieved March 23, 2004, from www.civilrightsproject.harvard.edu/research/disci pline/opport_suspended.php.

Irvine, J. J. (1991). *Black Students and School Failure. Policies, Practices, and Prescriptions*. Westport, CT: Greenwood Press Inc.

Joiner, L. L. (2002). Life-saving lessons. *American School Board Journal 189*(3).

Juvenile Crime Control and Delinquency Prevention Act of 2001: Hearings before the Subcommittee on Select Education of the House Committee on Education and the Workforce, House of Representatives, 105th Congress.

Katzenstein, M. F., and Reppy, J., eds. (1999). *Beyond Zero Tolerance*. Lanham, MD: Rowman and Littlefield Publishers.

McCarthy, M. M., Cambron-McCabe, N. H., and Thomas, S. B. (2004). *Legal Rights of Teachers and Students*. Boston: Allyn and Bacon.

New Jersey v. T.L.O., 469 U.S. 325, 342 n.8 (1985).

Public Law 101-647. (1990). The Gun-Free School Zones Act of 1990. 104 Stat. 4844.

Public Law 103-227. (1994). *Safe Schools Act*. SEC. 701, 20 USC 5961. Retrieved July 28, 2004, from usinfo.state.gov/usa/infousa/laws/majorlaw/gunfree/u20_8921.htm.

Public Law 103-227. (1994). Gun-Free Schools Act. SEC 1031, 20 USC 2701.

Public Law 103-382. (1994). *Improving America's Schools*. Retrieved June 25, 2005 from http://cc.ysu.edu/~cbvergon/PDFs/Discipline/us/gun_free_schools.pdf.

Reyes, A. H. (2001). Alternative education: The criminalization of student behavior. *Fordham Urban Law Journal 29*(2), 539–559.

Rimer, S. (2004, January 4). Some unruly students now face arrest, not detention. *New York Times*, pp. A1, A15.

Rosenberg, I. (2003). Random suspicionless drug testing: Are students no longer afforded Fourth Amendment protection? *New York Law Review 4*, 46 (3–4), 821–849.

Rumbaut, R. G. (2005). Turning points in the transition to adulthood: Determinents of education attainment, incarceration, and early childbearing among children of immigrants. *Ethnic and Racial Studies 28*(6), 1041–1086.

Skiba, R., and Peterson, R. (1999). The dark side of zero tolerance: Can punishment lead to safe schools? *Phi Delta Kappan 80*(5), 372–376, 381–382.

Snyder, T., and Hoffman, C. (2001, April). *Digest of Educational Statistics*. Washington, DC: National Center for Educational Statistics.

Texas Criminal Code. Texas Code of Criminal Procedure Article 15.27(a). (2000).

Texas Education Agency. (2000–2001). Safe schools. Disciplinary alternative education programs annual evaluation. Austin, TX: Author.

Texas Education Agency. (2002). *Comprehensive Annual Report on Texas Public Schools: A Report to the 78th Texas Legislature*. Austin, TX: Author.

Texas Education Agency. (2004). *2004 Accountability Manual*. Austin, TX: Author.

Texas Education Agency. (2005). *2004 Comprehensive Annual Report on Texas Public Schools: A Report to the 79th Texas Legislature*. Austin, TX: Author.

Texas Education Code Annotated. Vernon Supp. (2001).

Texas Education Code Annotated. §37.000. Vernon Supp. (2001).

Texas Education Code Annotated. §29.081(d) (6). Vernon Supp. (2002).

Texas Education Code Annotated. §36.001. Vernon Supp. (2002).

Texas Education Code Annotated. §37.000. Vernon Supp. (2002).

Texas Education Code Annotated. §37.001. Vernon Supp. (2002), p. 191.

Texas Education Code Annotated. §37.002. Vernon Supp. (2002).

Texas Education Code Annotated. §37.006 (a)–(d). Vernon Supp. (2002).

Texas Education Code Annotated. §37.007. Vernon Supp. (2002).

Texas Education Code Annotated. §37.007 (a) (1)–(3). Vernon Supp. (2002).

Texas Education Code Annotated. §37.007 (b) (A). Vernon Supp. (2002).

Texas Education Code Annotated. §37.007 (c). Vernon Supp. (2002).

Texas Education Code Annotated. §37.007 (f). Vernon Supp. (2002).

Texas Education Code Annotated. §37.008. Vernon Supp. (2002).

Texas Education Code Annotated. §37.008 (a). Vernon Supp. (2002).

Texas Education Code Annotated. §37.008 (a) (2) (A). Vernon Supp. (2002).

Texas Education Code Annotated. §37.008 (a) (4). Vernon Supp. (2002).

Texas Education Code Annotated. §37.008 (b). Vernon Supp. (2002).

Texas Education Code Annotated. §37.008 (c). Vernon Supp. (2002).

Texas Education Code Annotated. §37.008 (m). Vernon Supp. (2002).

Texas Education Code Annotated. §37.008 (1). Vernon Supp. (2002).

Texas Education Code Annotated. §37.011 (b) (1) (2). Vernon Supp. (2002).

Texas Education Code Annotated. §37.104. (2004).

Texas Education Code Annotated. §37.124. Vernon Supp. (2002).

Texas Juvenile Probation Commission. (2000–2001). *Juvenile Justice Alternative Education Programs Performance Assessment Report, 1998–2003*.

Tyack, D. B. (1974). *The One Best System*. Cambridge, MA: Harvard University Press.

U.S. Department of Justice. (1999). Indicators of school crime and safety. Retrieved July 29, 2003, from www.ojp.gov/bjs/pub/ascii/iscs99.txt.

U. S. Secret Service National Threat Assessment Center. (2000). Safe school initiative. Retrieved on August 29, 2005, from www.treas/gov/usss/ntac.

Verdugo, R. (2005). *Zero Tolerance Policies: A Policy Analysis in Draft*. Washington, DC: National Education Association.

Vernon's Ann. Texas C.C.P. Art. 45.055 (2005).

Vernon's Ann. Texas C.C.P. Art. 55.01 (Expunction of Criminal Records) (2005).

Will, George F. (2000, December 25). Zero tolerance policies are getting out of hand. *Boston Globe*, p. A3.

2

Student Discipline Removals: The Silent Cancer

Zero tolerance policies that suspend and expel students from school for serious infractions can be effective. More effective discipline is good for instruction and for good citizenship. It is the use of inconsistent implementation patterns that does not achieve its goals and sends the wrong messages. Instead of developing a discipline model that promotes the idea that more effective discipline is good and that discipline infractions have appropriate consequences, get-tough, zero policies send the message that arbitrary punishment for minor misbehavior is an appropriate goal. The original intent of Gun-Free Schools Act of 1994 was to expel students for bringing guns, other weapons, drugs, and tobacco to school (U.S.C, 1994). The federal code was used as a model for states to develop zero tolerance policies. The law focused on dangerous students, guns, violence, and drugs. At the state level, it has evolved into a policy that targets mooning, over-the-counter drugs, uniform violations, showing inappropriate affection, cigarette smoking, and school disruptions. This chapter defines zero tolerance theory, policies, and practices in the Unites States and Texas.

THE THEORY

According to some scholars, the policy for zero tolerance is grounded in law enforcement theory. According to Guinier and Torres (2003), education policy is one form of social policy that contains crime policy. In the 1990s a major demographic shift was taking place in the Unites States. Demographic shifts predicted that minority youth were gradually becoming the majority juvenile population in the Unites States. During this period, the media painted a picture of a wave of ruthless, lawless, fatherless, poverty-stricken juveniles without any morals or respect for the social structure. The media painted a picture of a wave of wickedness or a wave of youth with no respect for traditional social structure. This wave demanded a tough law and order approach (Mantle, Fox, and Dhami, 2003). School cases like Columbine only confirmed the need for the state to take control of student discipline in public schools.

Law and order theory specifies that the state has full responsibility for establishing the guilt and punishment of those who break the law (Mantle, Fox, and Dhami, 2003). Zero tolerance policies were incorporated into a national crime prevention effort with collaboration between the school districts and local law enforcement agencies. The national crime efforts focused on three major categories. The first category was the development of violence prevention and conflict resolution programs in school. For example, the Texas legislature mandated that all public school teachers receive training in mediation and conflict management. The Safe Schools Act of 1994 (PL 103-227) and the Safe and Drug-Free Schools and Communities Act of 1994 (PL 103-382) provided funding for peer mediation, conflict resolution, and other violence prevention programs (Casella, 2003). The second category attempted to mandate gun control laws. The Gun-Free School Zones Act of 1990 (PL 101-647) prohibited firearms within 1,000 feet of school property. The final federal crime prevention effort focused on punitive and judicial forms of school discipline. The Gun-Free Schools Act (PL 103-227) mandated that schools expel students for a minimum of one year for bringing a gun to school. The federal laws were tied to federal funding for public schools through the Elementary and Secondary Education Act of 1965. The ESEA of 1965 required that federal funding be withheld from school districts that did not enforce the PL 103-227.

Zero tolerance school discipline policies were elaborately designed as a response to school crime. The policies had three goals. The primary goal was to punish the offenders or those who broke school rules. The second goal was to use harsh punishment as a deterrent from further misconduct. The third goal was to separate offenders from the community (Mantle, Fox, and Dhami, 2003). Students who bring guns to school have to be removed from school for one year. Students are also removed if they bring other weapons, drugs, or tobacco. Removing guns, weapons, and drugs from school is important and necessary for a safe school environment. Student behavior is criminalized when policy makers acquire law and order theory and apply it to all school discipline policies.

States like Texas developed elaborate law and order discipline policies that outlined the list of crimes and the specific punishment that was to be applied by the degree of mandatory or discretionary punishment. The Texas zero tolerance policy is delineated in the Texas Education Code as "Law and Order." In addition to the state mandatory discipline code, policy mandated that every school district develop a code of district discipline policies. A six-year analysis of Texas discipline data shows that yearly an average of 17 percent of the Texas K-12 enrollment is removed from the classroom for some discipline infraction. These data do not include municipal court, county court, or state court discipline cases. Of all the Texas removals, less than 10 percent are mandatory removals. The remaining removals are for discretionary reasons.

Law and order theory professes that all are equal before the law and that those who break the law deserve to be punished. State zero tolerance policies mandate punishment that teachers and administrators have to enforce without consideration for individual circumstances or context. Theoretically, there are no grounds for discrimination or civil rights issues. If a student brings a knife to school, the student must be expelled; consequently, no consideration is given if the knife-like instrument is a finger nail file or butter knife.

According to law and order theory, punishment is more about teaching a moral lesson while serving as a deterrent to crime. Citizens are obliged to restrain self-interests for the good of society (Mantle, Fox, and Dhami, 2003). You cannot talk back to a teacher because she is the authority figure. The punishment for talking back to a teacher serves as a deterrent to future misbehavior or to deter future temptation to commit the same crime again. The moral lesson is that it is wrong to talk back to an authority figure. The key to law and order policy is toughness. There are no exceptions, considerations, or contexts for breaking the policy. Sociological and psychological issues should not be a consideration for education (Lezear, 2002). Law and order theory is not about teaching appropriate behavior or behavioral expectations. It is about conveying harsh punishment.

The language that the media used to convey the demographic changes in the juvenile population described changes in morality, race, and class. One newspaper article described the new juveniles as "fatherless, godless and jobless" (Butterfield, 1995, A18). One scholar described the new juveniles as "severely morally impoverished juvenile super predators" (Dilulio, 1995, 23). Dilulio implied that the new population, demographically African American and Hispanic, have a history of being criminals and will produce youth who are criminals. They will do what comes naturally: "murder, rape, rob assault, burglarize, deal deadly drugs, and get high" (Dilulio, 1995, 23). Some professional associations have recommended that schools use profiling as a technique for keeping schools safe (Joiner, 2002). Profiling in law and order theory refers to racial profiling. Profiling raises legal concerns concerning the validity and utility of profile measurement tools and their interaction with potential discriminatory practices, including search, seizure, and student privacy. Profiling on the basis of race, gender, or other personal characteristic bias has legal implications (Bailey, 2001). According to some scholars using the language of criminality to describe minorities has historical roots (Lopez, 2003).

Ian Haney Lopez (2003), in his analysis of how the Los Angeles law enforcement community used the language of criminality to depict Latinos, discusses how statistical and crime-prevention approaches figured prominently in the chief's philosophy regarding deployment in minority communities. If one uses objective, rational data, race-based differentiated policies are viewed as being fair and democratic. The following is a quote by the LAPD policy chief rationalizing the use of statistical policing and crime-prevention models:

> Every department worth its salt deploys field forces on the basis of crime experience. Deployment is often heaviest in so-called minority sections of the city. The reason is statistical—it is a fact that certain racial groups, at the present time, commit a disproportionate share of the total crime. Let me make one point clear in that regard—a competent police administrator is fully aware of the multiple conditions which create this problem. There is no inherent physical or mental weakness in any racial stock which tends it toward crime. But, and this a "but" which must be borne constantly in mind—police field deployment is not a social agency activity. In deploying to suppress crime, we are not interested in why a certain group tends toward crime; we are interested in maintaining order. (in Lopez, 2003, 135)

THE LAW

Zero tolerance policies were incorporated into a national crime prevention effort with three major categories. The first category was the development of violence prevention and conflict resolution programs in school. For example, the Texas legislature mandated that all public school teachers receive training in mediation and conflict management. The Safe Schools Act of 1994 (PL 103-227) and the Safe and Drug-Free Schools and Communities Act of 1994 (PL 103-382) provided funding for peer mediation, conflict resolution, and other violence prevention programs (Casella, 2003). The second category attempted to mandate gun control laws; the Gun-Free School Zones Act of 1990 (PL 101-647) prohibited firearms within 1,000 feet of school property. The final federal crime prevention effort focused on punitive and judicial forms of school discipline. The Gun-Free Schools Act (PL 103-227) mandated that schools expel students for a minimum of one year for bringing a gun to school. The federal laws were tied to federal funding for public schools through the Elementary and Secondary Education Act of 1965. The ESEA of 1965 required that federal funding be withheld from school districts that did not enforce the PL 103-227.

NATIONAL DATA

Research shows that school suspensions and expulsions produce negative school outcomes, such as lower achievement, dropouts, and racial disparities. In 2000–2001, 3,053,449 students were suspended in the United States (NCES, 2002). According to the National Center for Educational Statistics (2002) figures, national suspension data show that minority students are punished more often and more severely than majority group students. The data show that 6 percent of the U.S. public school population were suspended in 2000–2001 (NCES, 2002). Nine percent of all boys and 4 percent of all girls were suspended for the same period. While whites made up 61 percent of the total U.S. student population, they made up 15 percent of all suspensions. African Americans made up 17 percent of the U.S. student membership and 35 percent of all suspensions. Hispanics made up 16 percent of the U.S. student membership and 20 percent of all suspensions (NCES, 2002). The data lead one to conclude that minority students behave worse than majority students; however, those are assumptions. The law and order theory recognizes that all are equal before the law and that anyone that breaks the law deserves to be punished. However, there is evidence of race-biased differences in disciplining students, including data showing that minority students are more severely disciplined than majority students (Irvine, 1991; Wu Shi-Chang et al. 1982; McCarthy and Hoge 1987; Vavrus and Cole, 2002).

Data for Texas show that the greatest disparities between whites and minorities exist in subjective and more severe discipline categories like out-of-school suspensions and expulsions. Fewer disparities exist in the least severe and objective discipline removal categories; however, in every removal category minorities are disciplined more. In 2000–2001, African Americans in Texas made up 14 percent of the total state student membership, Hispanics made up 41 percent, and whites made up 42 percent. Low-income students made up 49 percent, and special education made up 12 percent. In the less severe short-term suspensions, 12 percent of the state membership was placed in short-term suspension. African Americans made up 23 percent of all the incidents. Hispanics made up 42 percent, and whites made up 34 percent. Low-income students made up to 58 percent, and special education students made up 25 percent.

While African American placements were overrepresented, the category of short-term, in-school suspensions exhibited lower racial disparities than the more severe out-of-school suspensions. In the more severe long-term and out-of-school suspensions (OSSS), 5 percent of the state membership was suspended from school. African Americans made up 32 percent of the removals, Hispanics made up 44 percent, and whites made up 24 percent of the OOSS. Of the OOOS, up to 68 percent were low income, up to 64 percent were at risk, and 31 percent were special education. African Americans were approximately four times as likely as whites to be placed in OOOS. Hispanics were approximately two times as likely as whites to be placed in OOOS. The more severe the punishment, the greater the disparity between minorities and whites. The most severe removal of expulsion showed the greatest disparities.

According to the research, zero tolerance policies are ineffective in promoting good behavior while creating negative consequences. According to law and order theory, punishment deters crime; however, zero tolerance does not work as a deterrent to misbehavior. On the contrary, in Texas, rather than decreasing discipline actions, the number of students and the number of discipline actions increased in most discipline categories over a six-year period. (See tables 2.1 and 2.2.) In discipline categories where the number of students have decreased, the number of placements or times the same student is removed have increased. Rather than serveing as a deterrent to misbehavior,

Table 2.1   Statewide enrollment data and student removal trends by students and by type of removal for 1998–2004

Year	1998–1999	1999–2000	2000–2001	2001–2002	2002–2003	2003–2004
State Enrollment	3,954,435	4,002,227	4,059,619	4,160,968	4,255,821	4,328,028
State Discipline Students	736,706	742,453	798,66	6619,823	644,092	743,643
State Placements	1,563,960	1,571,960	1,675,746	1,739,072	1,856,043	2,363,617
ISS Students	449,704	452,477	484,210	495,550	518,182	605,450
ISS Placements	1,095,334	1,098,010	1,166,604	1,185,759	1,257,572	1,611,960
OOSS Students	198,208	195,117	217,027	231,158	245,671	280,365
OOSS Placements	360,602	342,615	383,270	412,457	462,059	556,126
Expulsions/ Students	18,066	9,010	7,897	8,133	7,613	9,334
Expulsions/ Placements	23,044	9,750	8,220	8,823	8,068	9,993
DAEP Students	70,728	85,549	89,532	96,737	101,039	103,696
DAEP Placements	94,205	122,931	119,816	134,130	139,613	138,701
JJAEP Students	4,183	5,644	6,291	7,345	8,821	6,907

Table 2.2 Percentage of state enrollment by demographics and percentage of removals by student and type of removal 1998–2004

Year	1998–1999	1999–2000	2000–2001	2001–2002	2002–2003	2003–2004
African Americans in Texas	14	14	14	14	14	14
Hispanics in Texas	39	40	41	42	43	44
Whites in Texas	44	43	42	41	40	39
State Low income	48	49	49	50	52	53
State Special Education	12	12	12	12	12	12
Males in Texas	51	51	51	51	51	51
State Discipline Students	19	19	20	14	15	17
ISS Students	11	11	12	12	12	14
OOSS Students	5	5	5	5	6	6
Expulsions/Students	0.5	0.2	0.2	0.2	0.2	0.2
JJAEP		0.1	0.1	0.1		
DAEP	2.4	3.1	3.0	3.2	3.3	3.2

the law and orderlike policies resulted in a yearly increase in recidivism rates. (See table 2.4.)

Is there a relationship between suspensions and student achievement? While there are no empirical studies that answer this question, there are several studies that provide case data. Suspensions create disengagement from school and lead to negative school outcomes. When students are disengaged from the regular classroom instruction and instructional relationships, achievement goes down. When students are absent from the regular classroom, they get behind on assignments and lose important academic information. In a study conducted by Skiba et al. (2003), schools with high numbers of student removals had lower achievement. Elementary and middle school academic achievement and student engagement as exhibited by student misbehavior are predictors of early withdrawal from school and not graduating

Table 2.3 Academic excellence indicator system: 1998–2004; *Performance report for TAAS/TAKS percentage passing (sum of 3–8 and 10)

Year	1998–1999	1999–2000	2000–2001	2001–2002	2002–2003	2003–2004	2004–2005
**SAT TX	992	989	990	990	986	989	
**SAT US	1017	1016	1019	1020	1020	1026	

*AEIS, Texas Education Agency
**SAT1 Verbal and Math Mean Scores, *College Admissions Testing of Graduating Seniors of Texas High Schools in 2003*, TEA, 2004

Table 2.4   Type of removals and times student removed per student for 1998–2004

Year	1998–1999	1999–2000	2000–2001	2001–2002	2002–2003	2003–2004
State Discipline per Student	2.1	2.1	2.1	2.8	2.9	3.2
ISS Times per Student	2.4	2.4	2.4	2.4	2.4	2.7
OOSS Students	1.8	1.8	1.8	1.8	1.9	2.0
Expulsions/Students	.5	.2	.2	.2	.2	.2
DAEP	1.3	1.4	1.3	1.4	1.4	1.4

on time (Costenbader and Markson, 1994; Mendez, 2003; Orfield, 2004). In a study conducted by Mendez (2003), out-of-school suspensions climb each year rather than decline. Suspensions continued to climb from the fourth grade through the twelfth grade, peaking in the tenth grade. The study reported that even after the rapidly declining ninth grade enrollment in her sample, suspension rates continued to climb to 18 and 20 percent. Declines in the total school enrollment and suspensions were evident in the eleventh and the twelfth grade, suggesting that students experiencing suspensions dropped out of school before graduation (Mendez, 2003).

Texas discipline data for a six-year period (1998 to 2004) showed yearly increases in most discipline categories. Using SAT1 combined verbal and math scores as indicators of achievement, Texas achievement dropped slightly. Texas SAT1 scores from 1998 to 2004 dropped slightly from 992 to 989. During the same period, U.S. SAT1 averages increased from 1017 to 1026 (TEA, 2004).

STUDENT REMOVALS

According to Texas law, students are removed from their regular classroom using suspension or expulsion. Texas policies specify that students are suspended or expelled from the regular classroom into one of three alternative education placements. Texas student removal policy is designed to punish students for minor misbehavior by assigning them to in-school detention/suspension centers. If the student continues to misbehave or progresses to a higher level of misbehavior, harsher punishment is used. The student is isolated from the home campus into a disciplinary alternative education programs (DAEP). If the student misbehaves in the DAEP, or commits a high-level mandatory offense, the student is isolated in the county juvenile facility, the Juvenile Justice Alternative Education Programs (JJAEP).

The negative effects of zero tolerance policies have been shown to disproportionately affect minority, poor, and at-risk students, acting to segregate minority students and deny them the opportunity of an education. (See tables 2.5 and 2.6.)

In-school suspension units are used in the elementary, middle, and high school. Students are placed in a segregated facility on the regular campus. In-school DAEPs are optional programs, like a time-out center, a student assignment center (SAS), or a student referral center (SRC). An on-campus DAEP must use the services of a certified teacher. Regular classroom teachers send work to the isolation unit located on the campus for a short-term placement. While the discipline infraction is not considered a serious offense, the behavior requires isolation or punishment. The student offenses for this kind of isolation are clearly outlined in the student code of conduct as level I student offenses.

The second DAEP placement option requires that students be moved off campus to an out-of-school facility. DAEPs include district-wide, off-campus alternative schools for elementary, middle, and high schools. Students are reassigned or transferred to boot camp, district-wide DAEPs, and JJAEPS. Once a student is charged with a discipline infraction, he must complete the

Table 2.5   Student removal data 2001–2002

Removals	DAEP	Expulsions	OSS	ISS	JJAEP	State Data
State Enroll						4,059,619
All Students	89,532	7,897	217,027	484,210	6,291	798,666
Placements	119,816	8,220	217,027	1,166,605	6,832	1,677,911

Source: Texas Education Agency, Safe Schools Division

Table 2.6   Percentage of student removals 2000–2001

Removals	% DAEP	% Expulsions	% OSS	% ISS	% JJAEP	% State Data
State Student Removals	22	.2	5	11	.1	20
African American	21	19	32	23	26	14
Hispanic	43	47	43	42	45	39
White	34	33	24	34	28	44
Males	62	97	86	62	81	51
At Risk	54–64	54–69	55–64	54–61	NA	49
Low income	51–61	49–65	60–70	54–61	NA	50
Special Ed	25	26	31	25	NA	12
Mandatory	14		14		28	5
Persistent						
Misbehavior				52		

reassignment to be eligible to stay in Texas public schools. Punishment must be harsh and tough. If the student moves, he must complete the discipline reassignment in the new school. The only other option is for students to leave public schools and transfer to a private school, a charter school, or be home schooled. Off-campus disciplinary alternative education programs (DAEP) are used for discipline purposes including serious and persistent misbehavior, a felony, a serious offense at a school-sponsored activity on or off campus, and Student Code of Conduct Offenses (Texas Education Code Annotated 37.001 37.002, 37.006, 37.007, 37.008).

Persistent misbehavior is prominent in Texas zero tolerance. Persistent misbehavior is defined by the number of times an infraction is committed regardless of the seriousness of the offense. For example, in the local district, student code of conduct offenses are categorized from level 1 offenses in class, like cheating, unexcused tardiness, and failure to complete homework, to level II violations, which include inappropriate displays of affection, cafeteria disturbance, or uniform violations. Repeated disciplinary infractions for level I and level II offenses constitute persistent misbehavior. Level I and level II offenses are elevated to level III offenses and are reasons to remove a student into a DAEP for persistent misconduct. If the misconduct continues in the DAEP, students may be removed into the JJAEP. Some school districts define persistent misbehavior as repeating the same infraction five times or more. In the 2002 NCLB, legislation identified habitual offenders as "persistent" misbehavior.

The third and most serious DAEP option is placement in the JJAEP. The purpose of the JJAEP is to provide a placement for students who are on probation, on deferred prosecution, or placed by the courts. Students are also expelled to the JJAEP for the discretionary placement of serious and persistent misbehavior. A school district contracts with the JJAEP to expel students into the JJAEP. Placements are short term for less then ninety days or long-term for more than ninety days. Placements may be extended to 180 days with appropriate review. Data show that 52 percent of the state JJAEP placements in 2000–2001 were for the discretionary reason of persistent misbehavior. (See tables 2.5 and table 2.6.) Only 28 percent of the removals to a JJAEP were for mandatory removal policies.

SUSPENSIONS

Suspensions are removals from school generally for a period not to exceed ten days during an academic year. They are generally combined with denial of participation in the regular classroom activities. Generally, short-term, in-school suspensions remove the student from the regular classroom into an on-campus behavioral management center. Out-of-school suspensions are generally removals from the home campus to an off-campus facility, usually a DAEP, for a period not to exceed ten days or for a long-term, out-of-school suspension for a period to exceed ten days and as long as 180 days.

While suspensions carry due process rights, the procedure for in-school and short-term suspension is less court type. *Goss v. Lopez* (1975) rejected the use of courtlike due process procedures for suspensions. *Goss v. Lopez* prescribed an abbreviated due process procedure for short-term suspensions. The assistant principal, or another school official, immediately provides an informal hearing briefly informing the student of the offense and giving the student an opportunity for rebuttal. For a long-term, out-of-school suspension that exceeds ten days, a full due process hearing is required.

While suspensions are commonly used for school discipline, the national data show that suspension disproportionately targets minority students (NCES, 2001). In 2000–2001, African Americans made up 17 percent of the national public school enrollment, but they comprised 35 percent of all students suspended. Hispanics made up 16 percent of the national public school enrollment and 20 percent of the suspensions (NCES, 2001). Whites made up 61 percent of the national public school enrollment and 15 percent of the suspensions (NCES, 2001). In Texas, African Americans and Hispanics were generally overrepresented in short-term suspensions but overwhelming represented in the more severe, long-term suspensions. In 2000–2001, 11 percent of the Texas student population was suspended in school. In the same year, African Americans made up 14 percent of the student population in Texas, 22 percent of the in-school, short-term suspensions, and 32 percent of the long-term, out-of-school suspensions. Hispanics made up 39 percent of the student population, 42 percent of the short-term suspensions, and 42 percent of long-term removals. In 2003–2004, African Americans made up 14 percent of the Texas student population, 24 percent of the in-school, short-term suspensions, and 34 percent of the long-term, out-of-school suspensions. During the same period, Hispanics made up 42 percent of the student population, 44 percent of the in-school suspensions, and 45 percent of the out-of-school suspensions. Low-income students made up approximately 53 percent of the state population and approximately 69 percent of the in-school and out-of-school suspensions. (See tables 2.7 and table 2.8.)

In-school suspensions are considered the lowest level and the least severe form of student removal from school. In-school suspension facilities are located in the home school, allowing students to remain engaged in school. Instructional and peer relationships are maintained while students are removed from class for a short-term period. Students maintain contact with

Table 2.7   In-school suspension (ISS) data trends by percentages, 1998–2004

Year	1998–1999	1999–2000	2000–2001	2001–2002	2002–2003	2003–2004
ISS Students	11	11	12	11	12	14
Mandatory Placements				3	3	3
Special Ed Students	23	23	22	22	21	20
Special Ed Counts		25	25	25	24	23
African American	22	22	22	23	24	24
Hispanic	40	42	42	43	43	44
White	36	36	34	33	32	31
At-risk Students	57	57	56	57	57	62
Low income	57	56	58	58	60	62

their teacher, who provides them with daily instructional assignments. In addition, students are able to maintain day-to-day contact with peers. Table 2.7 shows that for the period of 1998–1999 to 2003–2004, state in-school suspension rates increased from 11.3 percent to 13.5 percent. Approximately 11 students per 100 state students were removed to in-school suspension from 1998 to 2004. In 2003–2004, in-school suspensions spiked to 14 students per 100 students who were placed in in-school suspension. Data for the number of in-school suspension placements show that from 1998 to 2004 every student that was suspended was suspended approximately 2.4 times. In 2003–2004, the number of in-school suspension placements per suspended student peaked at 2.6 suspensions per student suspended in school. The increasing number of students and number of times per student to be suspended is another indicator of the system's ineffectiveness.

Table 2.8   Out-of-school suspension (OSSS) data trends by percentages, 1998–2004

Year	1998–1999	1999–2000	2000–2001	2001–2002	2002–2003	2003–2004
Mandatory OOS				4	4	4
Special Ed Students	28	27	27	26	26	21
Special Ed Counts		32	31	30	28	28
African American Counts	30	32	32	33	33	34
Hispanic Counts	42	43	43	43	43	45
White Counts	26	28	24	22	21	21
At-risk counts	52	55	55	61	60	66
At-risk unknown	11	10	9	8	8	8
Low-income counts	55	58	59	62	62	62
Low-income unknown	11	10	9	8	8	8

In-school suspension rates by race show a disproportionate overrepresentation of African Americans and Hispanics. The in-school suspension rate for African Americans is much higher than any other group. Table 2.6 shows that for the period of 1998–1999 to 2003–2004, African Americans made up 14 percent of the state population and 22 out of every 100 state in-school suspensions. The in-school suspension rate for African Americans increased from 23 percent in 1998–2000 to 24 percent in 2003–2004. They were more likely than any other group to experience in-school suspension. Hispanic students made up 39 percent in 1998 and 42 percent of student population in 2003–2004. In-school suspensions for Hispanic students increased from 40 percent in 1998–1999 to 44 percent in 2003–2004. In-school suspensions for Hispanics were higher than the proportional student population for the state. While whites were not overrepresented in ISS, they had a higher representation in ISS than in any other student removal category represented in the Texas zero tolerance policy.

Special education students represented from 23 percent to 20 percent of the in-school students suspended from 1998 to 2004; however, they represent 25 percent to 23 percent of the placements. While the number of special education students is slightly decreasing over the six-year period, the number of times that a special education student is placed for in-school and out-of-school suspension is only slightly decreasing. Special education student in-school suspensions peaked at 23 percent in 1998–1999 and decreased each school year to 20 percent in 2003–2004. The special education group was the only group to see a decrease in in-school suspensions over a six-year period. The special education decrease of in-school suspensions may be credited to the aggressive lobbying of special education advocacy groups; however, it is still proportionally higher than the state special education population of 12 percent.

According to the research, low-income students are overrepresented in school suspensions (Mellard and Seybert, 1996). The Texas data on the removal of low-income and at-risk students show that no at-risk or economic status data were collected for 10 percent of all the in-school suspension placements. Theoretically, the data for at-risk and low-income students placed in in-school suspension is as high as 57 percent for 1998–1999 and as high as 62 percent in 2004. For 1998–2004, the percentage of students on in-school suspension increased from 11 percent to 14 percent of the state enrollment. From 1998 to 2004, the number of low-income students placed on in-school student suspension increased from approximately 57 percent to 62 percent. During 2003–2004, the number of low-income students placed on in-school suspensions was the highest for six years. Table 2.7 shows that during the same period, the number of at-risk students placed on in-school suspensions increased from approximately 57 to 62 percent. The data for low-income and at-risk status considered missing data or data not reported by the state. Low-income and at-risk students were the most adversely affected group of students to experience in-school suspensions. The data for in-school suspension placements and students show that minorities were overrepresented; however, the most grossly overrepresented groups for in-school suspensions were low-income and at-risk students.

OUT-OF-SCHOOL SUSPENSIONS

Out-of-school suspensions (OOSS) are generally removals from the home campus to an off-campus facility, usually a DAEP, for a period that exceeds ten days. Out-of-school suspensions are more severe than in-school suspensions because students removed from their home campus become more disengaged from instruction than remaining on campus for the in-school suspension. They lose contact with their regular classroom teacher and peers. Academically, they lose instruction and are unable to make up regular classroom instruction. This exclusion from the regular classroom has a negative affect on student achievement and contributes to student dropouts and not graduating from school on time. Out-of-school suspensions for a period that exceeds ten days require full due process procedures cited in *Goss v. Lopez* (1975).

Out-of-school suspensions create disengagement with school and instructional relationships. They correlate with many negative student outcomes, including students' poor academic achievement, grade retention, delinquency, dropping out of school, disaffections, alienation, drug use, and incarceration (Costenbader and Markson, 1994; Mendez, 2003; Rumbaut, 2005). Out-of-school suspensions, like most zero tolerance offenses, involve African Americans at disproportionately high rates. According to the research, African American students do not misbehave more frequently; rather, the research indicates that referral biases on the part of school administrators and teachers is more probable (Irvine, 1991; Skiba, 2000). Disciplinary practices are discriminatory because discretionary policies that are defined by terms like disorderly behavior or school disruptions are highly subjective. For example, in African American culture, youth's verbal sparring often turns into rough-and-tumble play that may be interpreted as school disruption, disorderly conduct of fighting, and a Class C misdemeanor (Henderson & Verdugo, 2002). This behavior presents grounds for criminal charges, school removal, and a class C misdemeanor. Embedded in this example is the lack of cultural and racial synchronization or a common racial and cultural identity with shared set of behaviors between students and teachers (Henderson & Verdugo, 2002; Irvine, 1991). The law and order theory of student discipline is grounded in traditional values that may be different from minority and low-income cultures contributing to cultural dissynchronization (Henderson & Verdugo, 2002; Irvine, 1991). This unfairly targets minority students and increases their representation in suspensions.

According to deficit theory, class and gender affect discriminatory practices of teachers toward low-income and minority students. According to Valencia (1997), teachers and administrators expect minority and low-income students to be low achieving and disorderly because presumably parents do not value education, students come from dysfunctional families, or students lack cognitive ability or the motivation to be good students. Another assumption is that minority and low-income students do not want to learn. Using the philosophy of zero tolerance, it is assumed that students who "interfere with the teacher's ability" to teach or with the ability of other students to learn should be removed from school.

DISCRETIONARY REMOVALS

The state data for the out-of-school suspensions treat minority students, particular African American students, more severely and with greater disparity than the in-school suspensions. They also cause a greater disengagement with education. During the in-school suspension, the teacher sends work for the student; consequently, there is a connection with the teacher, the school, and student friends. Out-of-school suspensions isolate students in an off-campus facility. The student breaks learning relationships with the regular classroom teacher and his peers. The data on out-of-school suspensions show that only 4 percent of all out-of-school suspensions during 2001 to 2004 were mandatory removals. The vast majority, approximately 95 percent of all out-of-school removals, were discretionary removals or removals left to the discretion of the teacher or school administrator. The number of students suspended out of school grew from approximately 198,000 to 280,000 during 1998–2004. Each student was suspended out of school approximately 1.8 times. African Americans are the most severely affected by out-of-school suspensions. They made up 14 percent of the state population and 34 percent of the out-of-school (OOS) removals in 2003–2004. In six years, African American OOSS grew from 30 percent to 34 percent of all OOS placements. (See table 2.8.)

Hispanics were also adversely affected by OOSS. The state Hispanic population grew from 39 percent in 1998–1999 to 42 percent in 2003–2004. During the same period, the OOS placements for Hispanics grew from 42 percent to 45 percent. Whites decreased in state population from 44 percent of the state population in 1998–1999 to 37 percent in 2003–2004. They also decreased from 26 percent of all OSS placements in 1998–1999 to 20 percent of all OOS in 2003–2004. Whites were underrepresented in state OOSS. Whites are more proportionately represented in the less severe, in-school suspensions.

As the OOSS rates for minority placements increased, the rates for low-income and at-risk placements also increased. The low-income OOSS placements increased from approximately 55 percent to approximately 69 percent from 1998 to 2004. The rates for at-risk placements increased from approximately 60 percent to 73 percent from 1998 to 2004. While the number of special education OOSS students decreased during the six-year period studied, the number of times each student was suspended to OOSS increased. Placements for special education students in OOSS decreased from 28 percent to 21 percent during 1998 to 2003–2004; however, special education placements only decreased slightly from 32 percent to 28 percent of all OOS placements. Special education placements per student increased from 2.3 to 2.7. Like the in-school suspensions, the OOSS data show a disproportionate number of minority, low-income, and at-risk placements. These data show that as the severity of the punishment increased, the disparities for minority and low-income students also increased.

EXPULSIONS

Expulsion is reserved for the most severe student disciplinary actions and represents the lowest number of removals. (See table 2.1). It is used when the student cannot be suspended into a DAEP. Expulsion involves denying a student an education for periods from ten days to one year. Since a person's education level determines what kind of job and income the adult will earn, education has property interest under the Fourteenth Amendment of the U.S. Constitution. When a student is deprived of property interests for more than ten days, procedural due process rights including a notice and hearing must be administered. *Goss v. Lopez* (1975) protects student property rights. In cases where the student's presence poses a continuing danger to persons or property or an ongoing threat of disrupting the academic process, the school may immediately remove the student without the due process procedures; however, it must be implemented as soon as possible following the removal.

Expulsion data show that minorities are disproportionately affected by the more severe discipline measure. In a six-year analysis of expulsion data from 1998–1999 to 2003–2004, African Americans made up 14 percent of the state population. During the period, expulsion placements for African Americans grew from 19 percent to 24 percent. Hispanic populations grew from 39 percent in 1999–2000 to 42 percent in 2003–2004. Expulsion placements for Hispanics increased from 42 percent to 50 percent. Expulsion placements for whites decreased from 33 percent to 25 percent. Whites were underrepresented in expulsion placements. At-risk students made up approximately 66 percent of the expulsions. Low-income students made up 49 percent of the state student population in 1999–2000 and 53 percent in 2003–2004. Low-income expulsions made up approximately 60 percent of 1999–2000 expulsions and approximately 70 percent of all 2003–2004 expulsions. The data show that of all the expulsions in 2000–2001, only 14 percent were for mandatory removals. The remaining 86 percent were discretionary removals that gave the school personnel the discretion to keep the student in school. Mandatory student removals increased to 25 percent in 2003–2004. The dramatic decrease in expulsions from 1998–1999 to 1999–2000 is attributed to the development of DAEPs in 1999–2000. See tables 2.1 and 2.9.

The data showed that the percentages for African Americans, Hispanics, low income, at risk, and special education increase slightly each year; however, the numbers were disproportionately higher than the state averages for the same categorical groups. An analysis of expulsion data for 1998–2004 showed that African Americans increased from 17 percent of all expulsion counts in 1998–1999 to 24 percent in 2003–2004. Hispanics increased from 45 percent to 50 percent for the same period. At-risk expulsion placements were the highest in this category, indicating a relationship between expulsions and student achievement. The more severe the discipline, the greater the disproportional representation of minority students.

Table 2.9   Expulsion data trends by percentages, 1998–2004

Year	1998–1999	1999–2000	2000–2001	2001–2002	2002–2003	2003–2004
Mandatory Expulsions		10	14	21	25	25
Special Ed Students		25	25	24	25	23
Special Ed Counts		27	26	25	26	24
African American Counts		17	19	21	21	24
Hispanic Counts		45	39	50	52	50
White Counts		36	33	25	26	25
At-risk counts	53	54	54	60	66	68
At-risk unknown	11	13	15	16	16	17
Low-income counts	49	51	48	49	51	53
Low-income unknown	11	13	15	16	16	17

SCHOOL DISCIPLINARY ACTIONS

Based on the Texas data, the 4 to 5 percent of mandatory suspensions and expulsions were objective and necessary. Theses removals provided a safe school environment for students and teachers. Mandatory removals meet the intent of the Gun-Free Schools Act of 1997. The concerns lie in approximately 95 percent of discretionary removals that appear to be ineffective and discriminatory. The data have historically shown that students subjected to suspension and expulsions are overwhelmingly minority students, low income, and at risk. A study conducted by the Children's Defense Fund (1975) reported that Hispanic and African American youth are suspended and expelled at overwhelmingly disproportionate rates, often unnecessarily. In 2000, the Harvard Civil Rights Project issued a study showing that children of color are disproportionately suspended and expelled. Data from South Carolina reveal that while African American children represent only 42 percent of the school enrollment, they constitute 61 percent of the children charged with disciplinary student code violations (Harvard, 2000). Texas data revealed that African Americans make up 14 percent of the state enrollment, but they constitute 24 percent of all student discipline violations. The Texas data also show that Hispanics make up 39 percent of the state enrollment but they constitute 44 percent of all the state discipline violations.

The data show that boys, particularly boys of color, are the most severely affected by student discipline. Nationally, boys are cited for disciplinary infractions ten times more than girls (Gurian and Stevens, 2005). According to the research, boys develop biologically different from girls, but schools are designed to fit girls' biological development. There is a need for adults working with boys to better understand the brain development of boys (Gurian and Stevens, 2005). In Texas, the most severe injustices are inflicted upon boys. Boys constitute 51 percent of the state data and 78 percent of all student discipline violations, including 97 percent of all expulsions and 86 percent of all out-of-school suspensions.

DISCIPLINE FOR SPECIAL EDUCATION

Discipline for special education students must adhere to federal policy like the Rehabilitation Act (Section 504), the Individuals with Disabilities Education Act (IDEA), and Americans with Disabilities Act (ADA). Federal legislation provides special safeguards for children with disabilities. Special education students have the right to a "free and appropriate public education in the least restrictive environment" (IDEA, 2004). Special education safeguards protect disabled students during the suspension and expulsion process.

Disabled students, like all other students, may be expelled or suspended for one or several periods that do not exceed ten days for the academic year without having to ask whether the misbehavior is a manifestation of the disability. Special education students may be suspended to an in-school placement in a Behavioral Adjustment Center (BAC), Student Referral Center (SRC), Student Assignment Center (SAC), or removed from the regular campus for ten days or less. Special education students may be placed in the in-school suspension facilities used by the school. The use of a time-out room accompanied by full IEP services provided by a special education teacher rather than an in-school suspension center may be equivalent to the regular classroom. The time-out placement may not count as a suspension.

Expulsion is categorized as a change of placement (34 C.F.R. 300.519). Generally, special education students may not be expelled or removed from their special education service or the Individualized Educational Plan (IEP) unless it can be shown that the behavior causing the disciplinary action is not a manifestation of the child's disability. After the IEP team has determined that the misbehavior is not related to the disability, a special education student may be expelled or suspended for a long-term period not to exceed forty-five days. The parent must agree with this change. Since all educational services cannot be completely terminated during a suspension or an expulsion, alternative placements must provide special education services. For example, if a student is suspended or expelled to a DAEP, a special education teacher must be available to work with the student. Texas policy requires that all DAEPs that enroll disabled students have a qualified special education teacher assigned.

In the case of a disabled student who is cited for zero tolerance mandatory removal infractions related to guns, other weapons, drugs, and bodily harm, the student will be immediately removed to the DAEP but will continue to receive full IEP services. The school is responsible for conducting a functional behavioral assessment and for preparing a behavioral intervention plan. Once the plan is developed, the IEP Team is responsible for implementing the plan and making modifications to address the behavior (34 C.F.R. 300.520). During that time, the IEP Team will determine if the infraction was related to the disability.

If the manifestation determination proves that the infraction was related to the disability, the student cannot be treated in the same manner as a non–special education student. However, the determination should not mean that the student is not subject to any discipline. Finally, if the parent does not agree with the removal, the student must be returned to the original placement (34 C.F.R. 300.520). If the manifestation determines that the infraction was not related to the handicapping condition, the student will be treated the same as a nonhandicapped student but must be provided with full IEP services.

Special education students make up 12 percent of the state population and 20 to 25 percent of all in-school suspensions, out-of-school suspensions, expulsions, and DAEP placements (See tables 2.7, 2.8, and 2.9.) In 2003–2004, special education suspensions decreased to 20 percent for the first time in six years.

DISCRETIONARY AND MANDATORY SUSPENSIONS AND EXPULSIONS

Mandatory infractions for which a student must be removed from school include committing a felony or misdemeanor; committing an assault or making a terrorist threat; using, selling, providing, or possessing drugs; using, selling, providing, or possessing alcohol, glue, or aerosol chemicals; public lewdness or indecent exposure; or committing a retaliation offense against any school employee (Texas Education Code Annotated, 37.006). Students must also be removed from school following off-campus cases such as when the student receives deferred prosecution for a felony, a court or jury finds that the student engaged in a felony, or the superintendent reasonably believes that a student has committed murder, manslaughter, or criminally negligent homicide (37.006).

Expulsion is a mandatory removal that represents a form of alternative placement that is combined with placement in the DAEP. Students committing serious offenses as defined in 37.007(a)(d)(e) of the Code must be removed and in most cases will be placed in the JJAEP. Serious offenses include possession of a firearm, an illegal knife, a club, or a weapon as defined in the Texas Penal Code (37.007[a] [1]). A student must be removed if the student engages in aggravated assault, arson, murder, indecency with a child, aggravated kidnapping, or conduct punishable as a felony (37.007[a][2][3]). Mandatory removal from the regular classroom and admission to an alternative educational setting is clearly or objectively defined in the Texas Education Code.

Zero tolerance policies were created to enforce mandatory student removals. Mandatory student removals spell out objective crimes for which students are removed from school. They are the most appropriate reasons to remove a student. Dangerous students who bring guns and other weapons to school do not belong in school. Students who bring drugs to school are a danger to students and teachers. They do not belong in school. Mandatory removals to the DAEP and JJAEP were developed for dangerous students committing mandatory infractions. If schools are to be safe environments, mandatory removals must be observed.

DISCRETIONARY REMOVAL

Discretionary reasons for which a student may be removed from the regular classroom into suspension, expulsion, DAEPs, and JJAEPs are removals that are assigned to the discretion of school administrators and teachers (Texas Education Code Annotated, 37.001). The Code defines some reasons for discretionary suspensions and expulsions. Section 37.006(a) of the Code provides discretionary removal or reasons for which a student may be removed from the home school into the DAEP for the following non–Title 5 off-campus felonies:

1. The superintendent or the superintendent's designee has a reasonable belief that the student has engaged in a conduct as defined a felony other than those defined in Title 5 of the Penal Code.
2. The continued presence of the student in the regular classroom threatens the safety of other students or teachers or will be detrimental to the educational process. (Texas Education Code Annotated, 37.007)

Chapter 37.007(b), (c), or (f) provides discretionary reasons for which a student may be expelled. Discretionary expulsions may be placed in the JJAEP based on the agreement between the county juvenile board and the sending school district. Chapter 37.007 introduces "serious and persistent misbehavior" as a discretionary removal option left to the discretion of the school district to determine actions for which a student may be removed.

The research shows that for minorities much greater disparities are found in discipline for the subjective charges of discretionary removals than the objective charges in mandatory removals, such as possessing drugs, guns, and other weapons (Irvine, 1991; Osher et al., 2003). Attitudes about race, class, and gender may cloud the subjectivity with which discipline decisions are made. The Texas data for 2003–2004 show that African Americans are four and a half times as likely as whites to be placed in long-term, out-of-school suspension. Hispanics are two times as likely as whites to be placed in long-term, out-of-school suspension. While African Americans made up 14 percent of the state population, they made up 34 percent of the long-term, out-of-school suspensions. Hispanics made up 42 percent of the state population and 45 percent of the out-of-school suspensions. The data show that 95 percent of all out-of-school suspensions were for the more subjective discretionary offenses. There were 605,450 in-school suspensions of which 96 percent were discretionary. The absence of absolute or objective definitions of misbehavior or disruptive behavior opens the door to discrimination in zero tolerance and other disciplinary practices.

CONCLUSIONS

While on-campus suspensions are the most flexible, they can lead to off-campus placements if misbehavior continues or is based on the infraction. On-campus program assignments may range from after-school assignments to three-days-or-more assignments to the campus Behavioral Adjustment Center (BAC), Student Referral Center (SRC), or Student Assignment Center (SAC), depending on the Student Code of Conduct infraction. While the student is in the assigned center, the student's classroom teacher sends daily work for the student to complete so that the student does not get behind academically. On-campus removals require that the teacher be certified and that the teacher maintain contact with the student. Upon successfully completing the assigned time to the center, the student may be returned to the assigned classroom. On-campus suspensions provide the opportunity to nip misbehavior in the bud. This is the opportunity to solve student problems by providing services they may need, including learning assessment and placement in more appropriate learning programs including literacy development, special services, and counseling. It is an opportunity to identify social services for the student and the family. This is an opportunity to identify students with serious behavior problems and placements in meaningful and well-staffed alternative settings.

The policy to remove students from their regular classroom is necessary for what the state and federal policy have identified as mandatory removals; however, it is bad policy for most discretionary removals or removals that require behavior, academic, or cultural modification. Student removals are contrary to the best educational practices. Zero tolerance policies set equal expectations on an unequal playing field, reject developmental needs of children, and deny educational opportunities by contributing to dropouts and poor achievement, while criminalizing student behavior.

Removal from school or from the regular classroom for suspension or expulsion goes against all the research and common knowledge about "time on task" (Berliner, 1988). School attendance laws are predicated on the belief that if a student is not in school, learning cannot take place (Achilles and Smith, 1999). Mandatory school attendance and keeping students in school have always been a national school policy (Alexander, 2000). The correlation among poor attendance, exclusions from school, and dropping out of school are only exacerbated by zero tolerance policies (Achilles and Smith, 1999; Harvard, 2000; Irvine, 1990; Skiba and Peterson, 1999). According to a Harvard civil rights study (2000), there are indications that removal from the regular classroom will cause students to drop out of school. The study reports that more than 30 percent of the sophomores who dropped out of school had been suspended. High school dropouts are also more likely to be incarcerated, creating the school-to-prison pipeline (Harvard, 2000; Rumbaut, 2005).

Zero tolerance policies that promote student removals are effective in reducing mandatory offenses but ineffective in reducing discretionary discipline infractions. If a decrease in the number of offenses is an indication of effectiveness, the data on the more serious mandatory offenses shows that there has been a decrease in the more serious mandatory offenses in the six-year period from 1998–1999 to 2003–2004. For example, murder decreased from 11 in 1998 to less than three in 2003–2004. Weapons violations decreased from 2,056 to 483. Illegal knifes decreased from 2,156 to 658. Firearms decreased from 1150 to 176. The data show that the more serious, mandatory criminal infractions decreased under zero tolerance policies.

The data for student removals for the same six-year period show that the number of students and the counts for removals increased every year for the period. In-school suspensions increased from 449,704 students to 605,405 students and from 1,095,334 removals to 1,611,960 removals. Out-of-school removals increased from 198,208 students to 280,365 students and from 360,602 removals to 556,126 removals. In the period of 1998–2004, the number of students who made up the state discipline data decreased from 18 percent to 16 percent; however, the number of times that each student was processed increased from 2.1 to 3.2 per student. These data are more indicative of an ineffective student behavior system and are more predictive of the uneducated rolls of American citizens for the next twelve years or at least through 2020 or longer if the system remains unchanged.

All the data on student removals through suspensions and expulsions show a disproportionate number of minority students who are the most severely affected by zero policies that disrupt their regular classroom instruction for in-school suspension and out-of-school suspension. The state data showed that the more severe the discipline, the greater the disproportional representation of minority, low-income, and at-risk placements; on the other hand, this study did not study the severity of disproportionality. For example, the suspension data show that in 2003–2004 African Americans represented 24 percent of all in-school suspensions, 34 percent of all OOSS, and 24 percent of all expulsions; however, the data for how many times each African American student was punished were not available from the state. The data did show that for all in-school suspensions, each student was suspended an average of 2.6 times. In OOSS, each student was suspended out of school an average of 1.98 times. For expulsions, each student was expelled an average of 1.07 times. Theoretically, some students could have been removed one time while others may have been removed fifteen times. In a study conducted by Mendez (2003), she found that suspension data showed that most students were suspended once, but African American male students were suspended more frequently or six or more times. Students who were removed fourteen times in one academic year were African American students in special education (Mendez, 2003).

Every year for six years between 1998 and 2004, approximately 17 percent of all the students in Texas, a disproportionate number of minority students, were negatively affected by discipline policies modeled after zero tolerance. Consider that 5 to 10 percent of all removals were for mandatory reasons with no other options and for the purpose of protecting teachers and students. It is not the mandatory removals that are a question, but it is the 90 to 95 percent discretionary removals that pose equal educational opportunity issues for minority students. The policies have a direct effect of disrupting education for one semester or one year when minority students are removed from the classroom and school. They have the indirect affect of labeling students as troublemakers regardless of the severity of the infraction. Academically, it is more likely that students will not survive classroom removal. They will get behind in class assignments, become school failures, and eventually dropout of school. One study showed that 30 percent of the students who drop out of school are suspended at least one time (Harvard, 2000). Was it the same group of students who made up the yearly 17 percent? Was it a different group each year? Was it a combination of different students and repeaters each year? The data do not show recidivism by individuals; however, the data do show that each year the recidivism for each cohort increases. The data are predictive of an uneducated Latino and African American population that will be creeping through American schools and into public life through 2020 and beyond.

REFERENCES

Achilles, C. M., and Smith, P. S. (1999). Stimulating the academic performance of pupils. In L. Hughes (ed.), *The Principal* (pp. 213–248). Upple Saddle River, NJ: Prentice-Hall.

Alexander, K., and Alexander, D. M. (2001). *American Public School Law*. Fourth edition. Belmont, CA: West/Wadsworth.

Bailey, K. A. (2001). Legal implications of profiling students for violence. *Psychology in the Schools 38*(2), 141–155.

Berliner, D. (1988). Simple views of effective teaching and a simple theory of classroom instruction. In D. D. Berliner and B. Rosenshine (eds.), *Talks to Teachers* (pp. 93–110). New York: Random House.

Butterfield, F. (1995, November 19). Crime continues to decline, but experts warn of coming "storm" of juvenile violence. *The New York Times*, p. A18.

Casella, R. (2003). Zero tolerance policies in schools: Rationale, consequences, and alternatives. *Teachers College Record 105*(5), 872–892.

Children's Defense Fund. (1975). *School Suspensions: Are They Helping Children?* Cambridge, MA: Washington Research Project.

Costenbader, V. K., and Markson, S. (1994). School suspension: A survey of current policies and practices. *National Association of Secondary School Principals Bulletin 78*, 103–107.

Dilulio, J. (1995, November 27). The coming of the super-predators. *The Weekly Standard*, pp. 23–28.

Goss v. Lopez. (1975). 419 U.S.565.

Guinier, L., and Torres, G. (2003). *The Miner's Canary: Enlisting Race, Resisting Power, Transforming Democracy.* Cambridge, MA: Harvard University Press.

Gurian, M., and Stevens, K. (2005, May). What is happening with boys in school? *Teachers College Record.* Retrieved June 21, 2005, from www.tcrecord.org.

Harvard University Advancement Projects and Civil Rights Project. (2000). *Opportunities Suspended: The Devastating Consequences of Zero Tolerance and School Discipline.* Retrieved March 23, 2004, from www.civilrightsproject.harvard.edu/research/discipline/opport_suspended.php.

Henderson, R. D. & Verdugo, R. (2002). Zero tolerance policies and African American students. *African American Education 2*, 39–62.

Irvine, J. J. (1991). *Black Students and School Failure. Policies, Practices, and Prescriptions.* Westport, CT: Greenwood Press Inc.

Joiner, L. L. (2002, March). Life saving lessons. *American School Board Journal 189*(3).

Lopez, I. H. (2003). *Racism on Trial: The Chicano Fight for Justice.* Cambridge, MA: Harvard University Press.

Mantle, M., Fox, D., and Dhami, M. K. (2003). Restorative justice and three individual theories of crime. *Internet Journal of Criminology.* Retrieved on August 6, 2005, from www.internetjournalofcriminology.com.

McCarthy, J. D., and Hoge, D. R. (1987). The social construction of school punishment: Racial disadvantage out of universalistic process. *Social Forces 65*, 1101–1120.

Mellard, D. and Seybert, L. (1996). *Voices about School Suspension, Expulsion, and Learning: A Report to the Kansas State Board of Education.* Lawrence: University of Kansas Center for Research.

Mendez, L. M. R. (2003). Predictors of suspension and negative school outcomes: A longitudinal investigation. In J. Wald and D. J. Losen (eds.), *New Directions for Youth Development: Deconstructing the School-to-Prison Pipeline* (pp. 91–120). San Francisco, CA: Jossey-Bass.

National Center for Education Statistics. (2002). *Statistical Analysis Report September 2002, Public Alternative Schools and Programs for Students At Risk of Education Failure: 2000–2001.* Washington, DC: U.S. Department of Education.

Orfield, G. (2004). *Dropouts in America.* Cambridge, MA: Harvard Education Press.

Osher, M. D., Quinn, M. M., Poirier, J. M., and Rutherford, R. B. (2003). Deconstructing the pipeline: Using efficacy, effectiveness, and cost-benefit data to reduce minority youth incarceration. In J. Wald and D. J. Losen (eds.), *New Directions for Youth Development: Deconstructing the School-to-Prison Pipeline* (pp. 91–120). San Francisco, CA: Jossey-Bass.

Public Law 101-647. (1990). Gun-Free School Zones Act.

Public Law 103-382. (1994). *Improving America's Schools*. Retrieved June 25, 2005, from cc.ysu.edu/~cbvergon/PDFs/Discipline/us/gun_free_schools.pdf.

Public Law 103-382. (1994). *Safe Schools Act*. SEC. 14601 (b). Retrieved July 28, 2004, from usinfo.state.gov/usa/infousa/laws/majorlaw/gunfree/u20_8921.html.

Rumbaut, R. G. (2005). Turning points in the transition to adulthood: Determinants of education attainment, incarceration, and early childbearing among children of immigrants. *Ethnic and Racial Studies 28*(6), 1041–1086.

Skiba, R., and Peterson, R. (1999). The dark side of zero tolerance: Can punishment lead to safe schools? *Phi Delta Kappan 80*(5), 372–376, 381–382.

Skiba, R., Simmons, A., Staudinger, L., Rausch, M., Dow, G., and Feggins, R. (2003 May). Consistent removals: Contributions to the school to prison pipeline. Paper presented at the Harvard Civil Rights Meeting on School to Prison Pipeline, Cambridge, MA.

Texas Education Agency. (2004). *College Admissions Testing of Graduating Seniors of Texas High Schools in 2003*. Retrieved July 28, 2005, from www.tea.state.tx.us/research.

Texas Education Code Annotated. §37.000. Vernon Supp. (2001).

Texas Education Code Annotated. §37.001. Vernon Supp. (2002), p. 191.

Texas Education Code Annotated. §37.002. Vernon Supp. (2002).

Texas Education Code Annotated. §37.005. Vernon Supp. (2001).

Texas Education Code Annotated. §37.006(a)–(d). Vernon Supp. (2002).

Texas Education Code Annotated. §37.007. Vernon Supp. (2002).

Texas Education Code Annotated. §37.007(a) (1)–(3). Vernon Supp. (2002).

Texas Education Code Annotated. §37.007(b) (A). Vernon Supp. (2002).

Texas Education Code Annotated. §37.007(c). Vernon Supp. (2002).

Texas Education Code Annotated. §37.007(f). Vernon Supp. (2002).

Texas Education Code Annotated. §37.008. Vernon Supp. (2002).

Texas Education Code Annotated. §37.008(a). Vernon Supp. (2002).

Texas Education Code Annotated. §37.008(a) (2) (A). Vernon Supp. (2002).

Texas Education Code Annotated. §37.008 (a) (4). Vernon Supp. (2002).

Texas Education Code Annotated. §37.008 (b). Vernon Supp. (2002).

Texas Education Code Annotated. §37.008 (c). Vernon Supp. (2002).

Texas Education Code Annotated. §37.008(m). Vernon Supp. (2002).

Texas Education Code Annotated. §37.008 (1). Vernon Supp. (2002).

U.S.C. Individuals with Disabilities Education Act (IDEA). (2004). Public Law 108–446.

U.S.C. The 1994 Gun-Free Schools Act. (1994). Section 921. Retrieved July 28, 2004, from usinfo.state.gov/usa/infousa/laws/majorlaw/gunfree/u20_8921.htm.

Valencia, R. (1997). *The Evolution of Deficit Thinking*. Washington, DC: The Falmer Press.

Vavrus, R., and Cole, K. M. (2002). "'I didn't do nothin'": The discursive construction of school suspension. *The Urban Review 34*, 87–111.

Wald, J., and Losen, D. J. (2003). *New Directions for Youth Development: Deconstructing the School-to-Prison Pipeline*. San Francisco, CA: Jossey-Bass.

Wu Shi-Chang, C., et al. (1982). Student suspension: A critical reappraisal. *Urban Review 14*, 245–303.

3

Disciplinary Alternative Education Programs

In 1995, Timothy Nevares, a tenth grader in the San Marcos Consolidated Independent School District, San Marcos, Texas, threw a rock at a passing car and injured a passenger in the car (*Nevares v. San Marcos C.I.S.D*, 1997). Although the incident did not occur at or near school, the Texas Code of Criminal Procedure, article 15.27(a), requires that school districts be notified of student criminal activity. The police offense report triggers school district action under the Texas zero tolerance policy, Chapter 37, Law and Order. In 1995, section 37.006 did not provide for notice to the student or a hearing prior to placement in a disciplinary alternative education program, regardless of length of removal. Section 37.006 mandates that any student who has engaged in conduct punishable as a felony "shall be removed from class and placed in an alternative education program." Timothy was removed from his high school and placed in the school district's disciplinary alternative high school program (named Rebound). Rebound did not have a library, and students were not allowed to take course books home. There were no extracurricular activities or student organizations, and there were no specialized science or foreign language courses. In fact, there was no real instruction; the teachers (not all of them certified by Texas teacher standards) simply assigned workbooks in class and loosely supervised these expelled students in an independent-study type of arrangement. The Rebound students, all of whom had been removed from the regular San Marcos schools, were required to undergo drug counseling. Drug counseling was required even when, like Nevares, their discipline problems or incidents did not involve drugs or other controlled substances.

Nevares' parents brought suit, conceding that he deserved reasonable punishment for his behavior, but arguing that the Rebound program was not a proper high school program and that it failed to present an "adequate" education, as required by Texas law. The federal district court agreed. It ruled that such removal of students from "regular high school classes for placement in alternative education [constituted] a form of punishment [to a program that was] not comparable to that received at San Marcos High School." Therefore, the court reversed the transfer, determining that it violated Nevares's due process. However, the Fifth Circuit Court of Appeals reversed the lower court's decision, holding that alternatives such as Rebound were a "mere transfer" that school districts could employ for disciplinary problems (*Nevares v. San Marcos C.I.S.D*, 1997).

What happened to Timothy Nevares is no longer the unusual occasion or extreme, which a number of critics noted at the time of the case. Rather, underachieving programs such as Rebound are now the norm for students considered as "discipline problems," "troublemakers," or "criminals." Moreover, these programs are not merely alternatives, like charter schools, home schools, and magnet schools that have arisen as alternatives to more traditional public schooling. Disciplinary Alternative Education Programs (DAEPs) provide a facility that punishes and isolates troublemakers from their peers. They serve as feeders into the school-to-prison pipeline. These programs have become criminalized, and the stealth employed by school districts and public authorities has allowed these alternative programs to flourish into a growth industry. There has been a convergence of large corporate interests, particularly the exponential increase in prisons and detention facilities throughout the nation and the burgeoning accountability legislation that has led to widespread standardized testing in the public schools. Thus, it has been in the interests of prison builders and detention facilities industries to exploit children's proclivities for defying authority and not fitting into societal expectations. Simultaneously, it fits the purpose of educators to remove troubled youth from school rolls, where their likely poor test performance will pull down averages. According to policy discussions, the theory is to interrupt the education of those students who do not want to learn so that that learning and teaching for others are not interrupted. This is more evident in states where financial resources and prestige factors determine the success of schools and school personnel. Overly harsh, state zero tolerance policies mandating disciplinary alternative education programs may be ineffective and often mean a transition from school into the prison pipeline.

This convergence has been long in coming but was never publicly debated or considered. It arrived on cat's feet, and obliquely, but it is clearly here to stay. Despite robust and longstanding debates, legislation, and litigation over such issues as school finance, vouchers, and desegregation, the public has never fully contemplated or acquiesced in this marriage of convenience that has led to the criminalization of school discipline programs and adolescent behavior. Moreover, it is not unexpected that the usual suspects would be involved in the process: African American and Latino boys, such as Timothy Nevares. It is particularly not unexpected that this phenomenon would thrive in Texas. Texas has a longstanding history of educational underachievement in its large African American and Mexican American populations. It has also served as the testing ground for national accountability movements. A study of the Texas student discipline system will have national implications and variegated local lessons. Regrettably, these lessons have come mostly at the expense of minority children. As examples of these issues have begun to surface, it is overdue that scholars and policy makers look at the decade of developments since the Nevares case and ask whether this is a direction that the nation wishes to travel. Any reasonable look at the phenomenon will answer this question in the negative. This chapter will discuss the development of Disciplinary Alternative Education Programs (DAEP) as an approach for isolating and providing a minimalist education for students removed from the regular classroom for zero tolerance policy infractions.

THE SEARCH FOR EDUCATIONAL EXCELLENCE

While the demand for educational excellence is a worthy goal, the absence of a vision for the public nature of education makes education a commodity available to the most knowledgeable, most aggressive, and better-financed consumer. Wealthy parents get to choose their schools by merely buying homes in the best school districts. Poor whites, African American, and Latino parents do not choose bad, urban schools or bad, rural schools; they simply cannot afford to choose better schools. They cannot choose to buy homes in the better neighborhoods. Under the educational excellence paradigm, schools become a commodity without a vision for the public nature of education. In a recent article in the *New York Law Review*, Frug (1998) proposes that, from its inception, public education has not merely been a market commodity parents provide their children. Public education had a social function. According to Dewey (1916), "each individual gets an opportunity to escape from the limitations of the social group in which he was born and to come into living contact with a broader environment . . . different races, differing religions, and unlike customs" that make up the American life (000). Public education was intended to be a public process in communities with many diverse people who have a stake (Frug, 1998). Public schools have the potential for preparing children for living in a diverse society; however, American schools face diversity by creating intellectual, social, and geographic boundaries that separate children along lines of race, class, and ethnicity (Frug, 1998). DAEPs are an example of education programs that act as disciplinary centers to separate high achievers from those students "not able to function in the structure of a regular setting" and who are disproportionately minority (Reyes, 2001; Texas Education Agency, 1998).

DISCIPLINARY ALTERNATIVE
EDUCATION PROGRAMS

DAEPs are products of zero tolerance discipline policies or the one-strike-and-you-are-out approach to school discipline. Zero tolerance means that the goals of the institution will not tolerate those who do not follow the policies and guidelines governing student behavior. The worthy intent of zero tolerance is to maintain safe schools by creating school discipline policies for students who bring drugs, guns, and other weapons to school (Gun-Free Schools Act of 1994). Students who bring drugs, guns, and other weapons, cause physical harm, or other crimes against students and faculty must be removed from schools for the protection of teachers and students. This proposes that schools must be safe environments; however, the scope of zero tolerance policies has evolved into all-purpose local school discipline policies and has criminalized what has historically been a behavioral development process.

DAEPs are an extension of zero tolerance policies that govern school discipline and outline student behavioral violations for removing students from the regular classroom, as in the case of Timothy Nevares. Students are removed using short-term suspensions, long-term suspensions, and expulsions. Historically, school discipline was completely governed by school principals and teachers using discretionary and police authority derived from the legal doctrine of in loco parentis and numerous legal decisions (Rosenberg, 2003). Long-term suspensions and expulsions provided a means for punishing students for severe misbehavior or refusal to obey reasonable school rules. Expulsion was reserved for the most severe measures in discipline actions, such as engaging in violence, stealing, or vandalizing school or private property, causing or attempting to cause physical injury to others, possessing a weapon, possessing or using drugs or alcohol, and engaging in criminal activity or other behavior forbidden by state law (McCarthy, Cambron-McCabe, and Thomas, 2004). In redefining school discipline policy and removing teacher discretion and flexibility from school discipline decisions, zero tolerance policy mandated behavioral infractions for which students must be suspended or expelled. Concerns that student removals amounted to nothing more than a vacation spurred the need for alternative school settings or isolation for behavioral management. Students who receive short-term suspensions are removed to a campus-based behavioral management center. Students who receive long-term suspensions or expulsions are removed to an off-campus behavioral management facility or a DAEP.

DEFINING ALTERNATIVE SCHOOLS

While there is no one commonly accepted definition of what constitutes a public alternative school, the more generic definition would include any learning experiences that are offered in place of a traditional school. Alternative schools are rooted in A. S. Neill's Summerhill School. The alternative school movement proliferated in the 1960s to include the Afro-centric school movement (Cohen, 1968). The alternative schools of the 1960s were innovative schools of choice. In 2002, the U.S. Department of Education defined alternative education school as a "public elementary/secondary school that addresses the needs of students which typically cannot be met in the regular school and provides nontraditional education which is not categorized solely as regular education, special education, vocational education, gifted and talented or magnet school programs" (Kleiner, Porch, & Farris, 2002, p. C4). This chapter focuses on the new-age, alternative school of the 1990s that is a non-choice, mandatory, placement school.

Raywid (1994) developed a model for defining alternative schools based on type I innovative programs of choice, type II disciplinary programs with mandatory placement, and type III developmental or therapeutic programs that provide academic and discipline support to students. Of the three types, type I, the more desirable model, focuses on student needs using individualized instruction. DAEPs were designed using a type II punitive model created to modify student behavior. The type I model assumes that something is wrong with an instructional program that does not meet the needs of the student. The type II model is a deficit school model. Something is wrong with the student or with the student's family. The punitive model has to be harsh and tough enough to teach a lesson to troublemakers. Placement in DAEPs is compulsory, and the only alternative is for a student to leave the public school system. Options include transferring into a private school, home schooling, or dropping out of school. Alternative schools have very different purposes. State policy may provide for a single, alternative school model while other states may have more than one model. For example, Texas has the innovative, alternative school model and two types of punitive alternative schools, the DAEP and the JJAEP. This chapter is concerned with the punitive DAEP.

Nationally, public alternative schools for students at risk of school failure have different purposes. Historically, alternative schools in the United States have taken many forms, emerging from innovative models of choice to recent mandatory discipline schools (Raywid, 1994; Young, 1990, 1992). The current DAEPs are sites that separate out at-risk, low-income, and minority students. Rather than using an innovative alternative school model that provides an education that meets the needs of students who do not function well in a traditional school model, a student deficit model was selected. Students who are unable to function in the regular setting are removed to a DAEP. The goal of the DAEP school model is to fix the student so that he can function in the regular setting of a traditional school. The theory of deficit thinking proposes that something is wrong with the student. The student fails in school because of internal deficits or deficiencies that over time have been identified as genetics, culture, class, and familial socialization (Valencia, 1997). Deficit school models fit law and order theory that proposes to teach a moral lesson about traditional values while harshly punishing and deterring future misbehavior.

Concerns have emerged that DAEPs represent a way to segregate minority and low-income students. Reports from North Carolina and Mississippi indicate that programs in those states have become dumping grounds for minority, low-income, and at-risk students (North Carolina Education and Law Project, 1997). Creating separate schools for minority and low-income students poses a major change in U.S. policy and the goal to provide an equal educational opportunity for all citizens.

In 2002, there were forty-eight states in the United States with alterative school legislation (Lehr, Lanners, and Lange, 2003). In 2002, Kleiner et al. reported that 39 percent of U.S. public schools reported administering 10,900 public alternative schools or programs for at-risk students during the 2000–2001 school year. They reported on a mix of alternative schools, including the punitive mandatory placement model or the DAEP. Urban school districts in the southeast with high-minority and high-poverty concentrations were more likely to report alternative schools; however, the alternative schools reported were more likely to be schools of choice. The study reported on some DAEPs. The Kleiner (2002) data were for schools administered by school districts and schools where students spent at least 50 percent of their instructional time.

Many zero tolerance policies require that a student be removed for 50 percent of or the entire school year for certain behavioral infractions. In addition, if a student is disciplined in the DAEP, the placement may be extended to as many as 180 days, or the student may be removed to the Juvenile Justice Alternative Education Program (JJAEP). The Kleiner data did not include private, for-profit DAEPs, like the Community Education Program (CEP).

CEP is a for-profit, alternative school program that contracts with local school districts (Community Education Partners, 2004).

There is much research on effective alternative schools of choice; however, that is not the case for disciplinary alternative education programs (DAEP). Kerka (2003) identifies eight factors that characterize effective alternative schools of choice:

1. a sense of community;
2. an assets approach;
3. respect for youth;
4. high expectations for academic achievement;
5. holistic, comprehensive, multidimensional developmental curriculum;
6. authentic, engaged learning that connects school and work;
7. support and long-term follow up services; and
8. caring, knowledgeable adults.

Other studies on effective alternative schools of choice identify characteristics such as low teacher-to-pupil ratios, highly structured classrooms, use of adult mentors, and social skills curriculum (Tobin and Sprague, 2000). DAEPs are grounded in law and order theory that does not incorporate the characteristics of an alternative school of choice. Law and order theory is not about teaching appropriate behavior or behavioral expectations. It is about conveying harsh punishment.

McGee (2001) reports that while students may get stigmatized as disruptive, deviant, and dysfunctional students for being placed in a DAEP, students can grow in a DAEP. Effective DAEPs are well designed with a friendly atmosphere and a high degree of autonomy with an equal focus on developing social and academic skills. Effective DAEP programs focus on the needs of the students rather than fixing the students. Programs in Pennsylvania identify the features of effective DAEPs as lower student-to-teacher ratios, customized curriculums, focus on social skills training and personal issues, and emphasis on discipline. Effective DAEPs use the more innovative model of alternative schools. DAEPs using the innovative, alternative school design should be the model for all DAEPs.

DISCIPLINARY ALTERNATIVE EDUCATION PROGRAMS IN TEXAS

Chapter 37 Discipline Law and Order, Subtitle G, Safe Schools of the Texas Education Code (TEC) was created to provide alternative settings for behavioral management with disruptive students in Texas. *Chapter 37* was the Texas zero tolerance policy that was developed for disruptive students. "Students not able to function in the structure of the regular school setting" must be removed from their regular classroom setting and placed in an alternative education setting based upon elaborate state and local discipline policies, rules, regulations, and procedures. Students were to be removed to DAEPs that were intended for students who commit crimes as outlined in the Texas Education Code. DAEPs are funded using state compensatory education funds theoretically intended to close the achievement gap for low-income students (TEC, Section 29.089). The theory for compensatory education was that students from low-income populations were the products of low investments in their health, housing, nutrition, education in the home, and other experiences enjoyed by nonpoor populations (Levin, 1975). The intended purpose of compensatory education was to provide "additional" investments in human capital for low-income students to compensate for the higher investments in human capital afforded to more advantaged populations (Levin, 1975). The intent of compensatory education funding was to enrich the educational environment for low-income students. It was never intended to pay for low minimal services provided by DAEPs. Paying for DAEPs with compensatory education funds takes money away from the intended purpose of enriching low-income students.

In 1995, Texas Senate Bill I provided policies that uniquely govern DAEP admission, teacher certification, curriculum, accountability, transfer policies, and student due process rights. DAEPs are different from the home campus because, until 2006, they were not required to use certified teachers, except for bilingual and special education—nor are they required to provide a class that a student needs to be promoted from one grade level to another grade level or is required for graduation (Texas Education Code Annotated, 37.008). The original intent of DAEPs was to provide a facility for dangerous and violent students. The DAEP is a prison model intended to isolate students from their community. Rather than the academic skills of a certified teacher, DAEP teachers need skills for controlling violent students or skills for controlling youth. It is the teacher's job to control the movements of violent offenders. Some of the original DAEPs used computer learning stations with a computer-based curriculum. Certification was not required. In an unpublished sample case analysis for a contracted off-campus DAEP, it was reported that out of thirty-one teachers, the principal, the English-as-a-second-language teacher, the special education teacher, and the career and technology teacher were certified. The remaining twenty-seven teachers were not certified. The teachers did have a bachelor's degree in law enforcement, sociology, health administration, business, social studies, general studies, and arts and sciences (Reyes, 2003).

There are districts that have responsibly provided certified teachers for DAEPs. The Austin ISD identified that 80 percent of the DAEP students were reading two years below grade level. Austin ISD thought it was important to deliver an academic program to keep students in school. The DAEP director said, "These students already feel alienated about education when they are sent out of their schools and they are further alienated when they are placed with unqualified teachers" (Reyes, 2003, 36). Timothy Nevares was not as fortunate. He was placed in a school without a library, without extracurricular activities, and without any extracurricular courses, even if they were needed for graduation. Most importantly, there were no certified teachers in the DAEP.

The DAEP has a minimum curriculum that focuses on English language arts, mathematics, science, history, and self-discipline while providing for behavioral and counseling needs. Timothy Nevares was required to go to drug counseling even though he had no drug violations. If a student needs a Spanish course for graduation, the policy does not require that it be provided. Spanish is not a core curriculum course.

DAEPs have a lower level of accountability and a lower level of state oversight. DAEPs are not required to meet the state accountability requirements except for students who are placed in the DAEP for the entire academic school year. Accountability scores for all other students are attributed to the school district rather than a home school. According to the law, removal of a student from the home campus to the DAEP is a transfer from one school to another school. By declaring that the removal of a student from the home school to the DAEP was mere transfer, student due process rights and accountability were minimized. According to state rules, when a student is transferred from the home school, accountability scores cannot be attributed to the receiving school (a DAEP or some other school) or the sending school. The accountability scores that belong to students who have transferred are averaged in with the school district totals (TEA, 2004).

The lack of accountability for DAEPs continues to be an issue. In a study conducted by the University of Minnesota, survey data for forty-eight states showed that DAEPs lacked clearly documented measures of effectiveness and student success or student outcomes (Lehr and Lange, 2003). While the No Child Left Behind Act (NCLB) compiles the Adequate Yearly Progress (AYP) federal evaluation of every campus, it does not extend the AYP to DAEP campuses. AYP evaluations are calculated using participation and performance on the state reading and math exams in grades 3–8 and 10. In addition, graduation rates and attendance rates are considered. The AYP evaluation rates are calculated using the Texas Assessment of Knowledge and Skills (TAKS), state-developed alternative assessment II, the locally-developed alternative assessment, and the Reading Proficiency Tests in English (TEA, 2005). Since there are no state accountability scores attributed to DAEPs or JJAEPs, there are no NCLB AYP evaluation rates.

In Timothy's case, the Fifth Court of Appeals said that no due process was required because Timothy was simply transferred from one district campus to another district campus (*Nevares v. San Marcos C.I.S.D*, 1997). According to the Texas Education Agency (2002), "the mission of alternative campuses is to enable students to perform at grade level"; however, there is no data to measure grade-level performance (p. 45).

The concern with Texas DAEPs is that a disproportionate number of minority, poor, and at-risk students are placed in these separate facilities with a lower-level curriculum. Historically, schools and administrators have been responsible for students, their behavior, and their achievement. When a student is transferred into a DAEP, accountability reverts to the school district rather than a school or an administrator. For teachers and administrators under the fire of high-stakes testing, the opportunity to remove a low-testing student off the school's rolls may enter into their decision to use discipline rules to remove a student.

PLACEMENT IN A DAEP

Students are removed from the regular classroom using student short-term, in-school suspensions, long-term, out-of-school suspensions, or expulsions. When students are suspended or expelled, they are placed in the DAEP. While it is unlikely that a student removed for a short-term suspension will be placed in a DAEP, schools do have that option. Students are more likely to be placed in a DAEP for long-term, out-of-school suspensions and expulsions. In most cases, short-term, in-school suspensions are student removals from the regular classroom into the in-school suspension center; however, there may be a case in which the student is removed for a period of less than ten days on an out-of-school, short-term suspension.

MANDATORY REMOVALS

Students are removed from the regular classroom into the DAEP based on mandatory or discretionary infractions. Mandatory infractions are those disciplinary infractions for which a student must be removed from the regular classroom into an alternative setting. Mandatory infractions give no discretion or flexibility for administrator decision making in school discipline issues. Mandatory infractions for which a student must be removed from school include committing a felony or misdemeanor; committing an assault or making a terrorist threat; using, selling, providing, or possessing drugs; using, selling, providing, or possessing alcohol, glue, or aerosol chemicals; possession of a gun or other weapon; public lewdness or indecent exposure; or committing a retaliation offense against any school employee (Texas Education Code Annotated, 37.006). Students must also be removed from school following off-campus cases for which students receive deferred prosecution for a felony, or a court or jury finds that the student engaged in a felony, the superintendent reasonably believes that a student has committed murder, manslaughter, or criminally negligent homicide (37.006). Mandatory infractions are the foundation of zero tolerance policy. In order for schools to be safe, students who bring guns, drugs, and other weapons to school should be removed. Students who endanger others should be separated. The intent of zero tolerance is to remove these students from school. This chapter supports the need to remove students for mandatory infractions. Schools cannot risk the safety of teachers and students. The Texas data on mandatory placements in the DAEP show that in the period between 1998 and 2004 less than an average 18 percent of all DAEP placements were mandatory placements.

There are two concerns with DAEP placements. The first concern is that 82 percent of all Texas DAEP placements were discretionary placements. How many of the discretionary placements were for horsing around or for not having the skills to complete homework or class assignments? The second concern with DAEPs is mixing students who committed minor discretionary offenses with students who committed dangerous mandatory crimes in the same facility.

Expulsion is a mandatory removal that represents a form of alternative placement that is combined with placement in the DAEP, JJAEP, or home. Students committing serious offenses as defined in TEC 37.007(a), (d), (e) must be removed and in most cases will be placed in the DAEP or JJAEP. Serious offenses include possession of a firearm, an illegal knife, a club, or a weapon as defined in the TEC (37.007[a][1]). A student must be removed if the student engages in aggravated assault, arson, murder, indecency with a child, aggravated kidnapping, or conduct punishable as a felony (37.007[a][2][3]). Mandatory expulsion from the regular classroom and admission to an alternative educational setting is clearly or objectively defined student infraction.

Mandatory removals define violent and criminal behavior for which a student must be removed from the school. Mandatory removals define the philosophy and the impetus of zero tolerance. Dangerous students should be removed from school to make schools safe environments. The fear of Columbine, the fear of a student running through a school shooting down students and teachers defines zero tolerance. The fear that students with guns, knives, and other weapons are dangerous and violent guided the philosophy of zero tolerance. The Texas Education Code clearly defined violent acts and violent behavior. In practice, DAEP student enrollment data show that for the period of 1998 to 2001, only 14 to 16 percent of all the students placed in a DAEP were placed for mandatory reasons. A six-year analysis of DAEP removals show that from 1998 to 2004, mandatory removals have increased from 14 percent to 23 percent or an average of 18 percent. DAEPs in Texas were intended to be facilities for mandatory removals. (See table 3.1.)

DISCRETIONARY REMOVAL TO DAEP

Discretionary infractions are those infractions left to the discretion of district administrators and teachers to define as discretionary in the school district student code of conduct (TEC, 37.001). Within the category of discretionary student removals, a school district may designate local mandatory student removals in the local student code of conduct. While the district may develop their own category of mandatory infractions in the student code of conduct, the state policy may recognize these infractions as discretionary (TEC, 37.001). For example, a district may decide that mooning and the inappropriate use of

Table 3.1   Disciplinary Alternative Education Programs (DAEP) percentages for 1998–2004

Year	1998–1999	1999–2000	2000–2001	2001–2002	2002–2003	2003–2004
State Population Percentage	18	21	22	22	23	23
Mandatory Placements	14	16	15	19	20	23
Males	74	ND	74	ND	73	ND
Special Education Students	25	25	25	25	24	23
Special Education Placements	28	26	25	25	25	25
African Americans	21	23	21	22	22	23
Hispanics	41	41	43	44	46	46
Whites	37	35	34	33	31	29
At-Risk Placements	53	55	55	60	63	69
At-Risk Missing	10	7	10	9	9	9
Low Income	51	51	55	53	56	57
Low-Income Missing	9	7	10	9	9	9

food are mandatory infractions requiring the removal of a student into a DAEP; however, this is not a mandatory infraction in state policy.

In addition, section 37.006(a) of the TEC provides discretionary removal or reasons for which a student may be removed from the home school into the DAEP for the following non–Title 5, off-campus felonies:

1. The superintendent or the superintendent's designee has a reasonable belief that the student has engaged in a conduct as defined a felony offense other than those defined in Title 5 of the Penal Code.
2. The continued presence of the student in the regular classroom threatens the safety of other students or teachers or will be detrimental to the educational process. (Texas Education Code Annotate, 37.007)

TEC Section 37.007 introduces "serious and persistent misbehavior" as a discretionary expulsion option left to the discretion of the school district to determine actions for which a student may be removed. School districts have the discretion to develop the student code of conduct that outlines student infractions, disciplinary options, and student placements (Texas Education Code Annotated, 37.001). A review of the code of conduct for a large, Texas urban school district revealed that district's definition of "serious and persistent misbehavior" created a subjective discipline category that adversely affects the removal of low-income, at-risk, and minority students from the regular classroom into the DAEP and into the JJAEP (Reyes, 2001).

Serious and persistent misbehavior is defined by the number of times an infraction is committed regardless of the seriousness of the offense. For example, in the student code of conduct, offenses are categorized from level 1 offenses in class like cheating, unexcused tardiness, copying, and failure to complete homework. Level II violations include inappropriate display of affection, cafeteria disturbance, failure to deliver or return written communications between home and school, or uniform violations. Repeated disciplinary infractions for level I and level II offenses constitute serious and persistent misbehavior. Some school districts define persistent as repeating the same infraction five times or more. Level I and level II infractions are elevated to level III infractions and qualify a student for removal into a DAEP. If the behavior continues, the student may be removed into a JJAEP. JJAEPs are reserved for the most serious crimes, including students on probation, students on deferred prosecution, or students placed by a court order. A student who may be nonliterate and continuously fails to complete homework may end up in a facility reserved for serious crimes.

Discretionary student placements into the DAEP averaged 85 percent of all DAEP placements in the period from 1998 to 2001. From 2001–2002 to

2003–2004, discretionary removals decreased from 81 percent to 77 percent. Serious and persistent misbehavior placements into the DAEP are reported as violation of the student code of conduct rules for five times or more. The degree of misbehavior is not an issue for a student to be placed into a DAEP for serious and persistent misbehavior. For example, level I student-code-of-conduct infractions are the lowest level of misbehavior; however, if the student persistently or for five times or more commits a level I infraction, the student may be removed to the DAEP. If the misbehavior continues in the DAEP, the district may remove the student into the JJAEP. State data for 1998 to 2001 identified an average of 10 percent of all DAEP placements that were removed from the DAEP into the JJAEP for serious and persistent misconduct or violation of the student code of conduct while placed in the DAEP (TEA, 2002). State data also showed that 52 percent of all JJAEP placements were for serious and persistent misbehavior (Texas Juvenile Probation Commission, 2002).

DAEPs are intended for mandatory student removals for criminal activity. In a six-year period, an average of 18 percent of the student removals met the intent and the purpose of DAEPs. It is possible there was a mismatch between 78 percent of the DAEP placements and the DAEP program design. The data show that approximately 78 percent of DAEP students were at risk of dropping out of school, an indicator that, for many DAEP students, literacy and learning are a problem. The punitive DAEP model was intended to punish students and not to provide remediation or to increase literacy skills.

SCHOOL DISTRICT STUDENT CODE OF CONDUCT

The state definition of mandatory reasons for which a student must and may be removed from the regular classroom and admitted into the alternative setting are generally very objective. Discretionary removal is more subjective. For example, an African American teacher may see two African American students horse playing. She understands the activity as horsing around and common to African American students (Irvine, 1991). The same activity when viewed by a teacher unfamiliar with African American cultural and structural paradigms may be viewed as school disruption and a class C misdemeanor of fighting. Verdugo (2002) provides an analysis of cultural and structural paradigms with educational consequences and school solutions. Irvine (1999) provides resources for cultural synchronization with African American students. African American and Hispanic structural and cultural paradigms represent classroom management content that teachers need.

EXITING FROM DAEP

In order to return to the home campus, a DAEP student must successfully serve their time in the program. Some districts, like the Austin Independent School District, condition exit from the DAEP, upon completion of the program's cycle of academic and behavioral modifications rather than time served. Students in a DAEP may be assigned for up to 180 days. In serious cases, students may continue from one year to the next in a DAEP. After 120 days, a student review is required as a way to provide some due process (TEC, 37.000); this is roughly more than one semester.

DISPROPORTIONATE ENROLLMENT OF MINORITIES, LOW-INCOME, AND AT-RISK STUDENTS

Nationally, the concern with zero tolerance is the disproportionate enrollment of minority, low-income, and at-risk students. The concern extends to Disciplinary Alternative Education Programs that provide low-level, minimal instructional programs by teachers who may not be certified, except in the case of the English-as-a-second-language (ESL) teacher and the special education teacher. DAEP can meet this requirement by showing that they have one certified ESL teacher and one certified special education teacher.

African Americas are most severely affected by DAEPs in the elementary grades where their enrollments in DAEPs are the highest. DAEP enrollment for African Americans decreases in the secondary grades. In 2003–2004, African Americans in Texas made up 14 percent of the state enrollment in grades K–5. For the same period, they made up an average of 35 percent of the DAEP enrollment in the first through fifth grade. In 2003–2004, African Americans made up 14 percent of the state enrollment in the sixth through twelfth grade. For the same period, they made up about 21 percent of the DAEP enrollment per grade level for grades 6 to 12. (See table 3.2.)

The disproportionately high enrollment of African American students in elementary DAEP programs is an indication of conflict between the values of zero tolerance policies and students. It shows a socialization conflict between teachers and students. Those who use a deficit school model blame parents for the students' lack of social and academic preparation for school. Some assume that parents do not have an appreciation for an education. Parents have not provided traditional social values for their children, such as reliability, loyalty, and capacity to take directions. The assumption is that learning is an absorption process that occurs from passively sitting and listening. Children should come to school with the right work and discipline ethic. Deficit school models blame the student and the family. In many cases, it may be that teachers do not have the classroom management skills or student background knowledge (Irvine, 1991; Verdugo, 2002). For example, the analysis of discipline referrals for one first grade teacher in Texas showed that she made fifty-two discipline referrals. Of the fifty-two referrals, fifty were for one African American male. The following year, the child was placed with another teacher and received no discipline referrals.

In 2003–2004, Texas Hispanic students comprised 44 percent of the K–12 enrollment, with the heaviest concentration of students in the elementary grades. They comprise 47 percent in the first grade, 45 percent in the second grade, 44 percent in the third grade, 43 percent in the fourth grade, and 42 percent in the fifth grade. The state Hispanic student enrollment drops from 42 percent in the ninth grade to 33 percent in the twelfth grade. The Hispanic DAEP enrollment ranges from 31 percent in the first grade to 37 percent in the fifth grade. The Hispanic state middle school enrollment ranges from 42 percent in the sixth grade to 40 percent in the eighth grade. As the Hispanic state enrollment decreases, the Hispanic DAEP enrollment increases at a disproportionately high rate. Hispanic DAEP enrollment ranges from 48 percent in the sixth grade to 50 percent in the eighth grade. High Hispanic DAEP enrollments in the middle school may be a reflection of low literacy skills that become more evident in the ninth grade along with high school retention rates, and high school overage or aging out of high school (Orfield, 2004; Reyes, 2004). In a study of urban principals in high Hispanic enrollment high schools, principals reported that the ninth grade was the most challenging grade level. Almost 25 percent of the Hispanic students entering the ninth grade were nonliterate. In addition, the ninth grade hosted a cohort of new immigrant students who spoke only Spanish. A third category of students was the overage ninth graders who were twenty-one years old and did not have enough credits to be placed in the tenth grade. Students who do not have the literacy skills to participate in the learning process become discipline problems, as the Hispanic DAEP enrollment data for sixth, seventh, eighth, ninth, and tenth grade show.

The high school data identify Hispanic literacy issues. According to the principals in this study, Hispanic students are placed in short-term, bilingual/ English-as-a-second-language programs in the elementary level. The pressure to move students into an English program and to test in English forces an early exit from Bilingual/ESL programs. Elementary bilingual/ESL students are exited from programs before they are literate. They have learned enough English to survive the fourth and fifth grade. Principals commented that students who were promoted to the sixth grade and were seen in the neighborhood did not enroll for the sixth grade in middle school. By middle school, low literacy levels are evident in academic struggles. Students who struggle academically, drop out by the sixth grade or become discipline problems. According to a municipal teen court judge, 80 percent of the students that schools referred to him for class C misdemeanors of school disruption could not read English.

The state Hispanic student enrollment increases from 40 percent in the eighth grade to 42 percent in the ninth grade. The Hispanic ninth grade DAEP enrollment peaks at 50 percent. The ninth grade, Hispanic state enrollment increase is not an increase in the number of students. Rather, it is a reflection of a concentration of students who are repeatedly retained in the ninth grade. The ninth grade is the second major high school dropout phase. The true ninth grade enrollment would be higher if it were not for the number of students who are weeded out of school or drop out of school in the ninth grade. The ninth grade serves as a warehouse for overage and nonliterate Hispanic students who will drop out of school or get a GED before they reach the twelfth grade. It is also the beginning of the third phase of the Hispanic student dropout process. Hispanics decrease from a 42 percent enrollment in the ninth grade to a 34 percent enrollment in the twelfth grade. As the state Hispanic student enrollment decreases, the DAEP Hispanic student enrollment levels off from 50 percent to 32 percent. DAEP enrollment may be related to Hispanic student enrollment decreases and dropping out of school.

The Texas data, as shown in table 3.2, reflects the negative affects of DAEP on Hispanic students. The Harvard civil rights study (2000) and Orfield

Table 3.2   DAEP enrollment by grade level, 2003–2004*

GR	State	DAEP Hispanic	State	DAEP Afr Am	DAEP Low Income
1	46.5	30.8	13.5	37.1	66.2
2	45.6	34.4	13.9	36.5	69.0
3	44.7	32.6	14.4	38.4	71.5
4	43.6	37.2	14.6	34.8	70.2
5	42.6	37.0	14.5	33.4	71.5
6	41.8	47.5	14.7	26.3	69.6
7	40.7	50.5	14.6	22.5	64.7
8	39.8	50.3	14.5	20.0	59.7
9	42.1	49.5	15.0	20.8	52.4
10	38.1	42.2	14.5	21.3	44.2
11	35.4	36.4	13.7	20.1	38.0
12	33.9	31.9	13.3	19.6	33.2

*2004 Comprehensive Report on Texas Public Schools, Texas Education Agency

(2004) show that school removals cause students to drop out of school. Low-income students were the most adversely affected students. While the average data show that 59 percent of all DAEP enrollments were low income, the enrollment data for the first grade through the ninth grade show that 66 percent were low income. Grade level data for low-income students show that the highest enrollment of low-income students occurs in the lower grades, gradually decreasing to 33 percent in the twelfth grade.

The DAEP table 3.1 enrollment data from 1998 to 2004 show that African Americans and Hispanics are overrepresented in DAEP placements and whites are underrepresented. According to the table, DAEP placements for Hispanics and African Americans had a steady increase in placements over the six-year period. In 2003–2004, African Americans were 2.19 times more likely to be placed in a DAEP than whites. Hispanics were 1.41 times more likely to be placed in a DAEP than whites. During the six-year period analyzed, DAEP student enrollments grew approximately 32 percent, while the state student population only grew 12 percent (TEA, 2005 March).

JJAEP ENROLLMENTS

JJAEP enrollment data in table 3.3 showed that in Texas approximately 5,900 to 6,900 placements were made into the JJAEP from 2000 to 2004. JJAEPs are reserved for the most severe school criminal infractions. The JJAEPs are

Table 3.3 Juvenile Justice Alternative Education Programs (JJAEP) percentages, 1998–2004

Year	1998–1999	1999–2000	2000–2001	2001–2002	2002–2003	2003–2004
State Population Percentage				.1	.1	.1
Mandatory Placements		25	28	21	27	26
Discretionary						60
Other						14
Males			81			81
Persistent Misbehavior			52			48
Special Education Students		19	21	24	23	26
Special Education Placements	28	26	25	25	25	25
African Americans			21	26	27	26
Hispanics			43	50	50	49
Whites			34	23	24	24
At-Risk Placements						81
Low-Income						59

selectively required for large urban environments where 125,000 or more citizens reside in a county. They are not required for smaller communities. The assumption is that student crime exists in large, urban, primarily minority, communities. JJAEPs are sponsored by the County Juvenile Justice Board and may be housed in juvenile facilities that are jail-like, for those students who are incarcerated. The qualities of JJAEP educational services are more minimal than the DAEP, with fewer qualified teachers. The JJAEP may use itinerant certified personnel to meet the special education and ESL teacher requirements. In the state of Texas, only 18 percent of the teachers who teach in JJAEPs have teacher certification.

JJAEP crimes include drugs, weapons, murder, parole violations, assaults, and felonies. These are all infractions that require mandatory placement in a JJAEP. The data show that mandatory infractions represent approximately 25 percent of all JJAEP placements, 60 percent of which are discretionary placements, with the remaining placements including court appointments and other placements. JJAEPs have contractual agreements with local school districts for the placement of students who are categorized as serious and persistent misbehavior. The JJAEP data show that 48 to 55 percent of the JJAEP placements are for serious and persistent misbehavior contracts with local school districts.

JJAEP enrollments show that minority, low-income, at-risk, and male students were overrepresented in the JJAEP. In 2003–2004, African American students made up 14 percent of the state population and 24 percent of the JJAEP enrollment. Low-income students made up 52 percent of the state population and 58 percent of the JJAEP enrollment. At-risk students made up 81 percent of all JJAEP. Male students made up 81 percent of JJAEP enrollments. African American students are 2.6 times as likely as whites to be placed in the JJAEP. Hispanics are 1.75 times as likely as whites to be placed in the JJAEP.

RACE AS AN ISSUE IN STUDENT DISCIPLINE

The data on student suspensions and expulsions into the DAEPs and JJAEPs show a disproportionate number of minority students who are most severely affected by zero tolerance policies that disrupt their regular classroom instruction and their opportunity for an education. Classroom removals lead to students falling behind in their courses, poor grades, and dropping out of school. The disproportional representation of minorities in DAEPs shows that race, class, and gender are issues in student discipline consequences; however, teachers and principals never talk about race. While teachers and principals do not talk about race as a discipline issue, one judge interviewed did talk frankly about race. He commented that of the eighty school discipline cases per week for which he is responsible, 80 percent are immigrant students who are nonliterate (Interview with David Fraga, December 2004). According to Pollock (2004), Americans do not know when or how to talk about people in racial terms for fear that race conversations will reinforce racism. In a study conducted by Pollock (2004), she discovered six core dilemmas of American race talk. She also found ways that educators and policymakers might engage in constructive conversations about race. Pollock asserts that identifying racial patterns in racial achievement is only the first step in solving the problem. Identifying the racial patterns in student zero tolerance policies, as this chapter does, is a first step to seeking solutions to an ineffective student discipline system. As Pollock points out, the second step is for Americans inside and outside of schools to look at their own roles in creating patterns of criminalizing student behavior as early as the first grade. Americans need to look at the role they play in creating patterns of disproportionate representation of minority students in student removals from their regular classroom and out of the school. State policy punishes students and teachers because they cannot fix school student behavior. So, they use school violence policies that only create societal disparities. Not talking about race and its affect on educational opportunity and the development of good citizenship is only more detrimental.

While race is an unavoidable issue in zero tolerance policies, other issues include the affects of high-stakes testing on teachers and principals. Testing has forced teachers to dedicate school time to test preparation time. Historically, principals and teachers were responsible for instruction and student behavior. They were properly prepared on an ongoing basis to manage their classroom and their students. As student populations became more diverse, the task became more challenging, but with ongoing support and time to develop student and parent relationships, student discipline was manageable. In a test-driven environment, time for relationships with students and parents has been sacrificed. The data in this book provide guidance for a reevaluation of the long-term consequences to minority, low-income, and male citizens.

REFERENCES

Cohen, D. K. (1968). Policy for the public schools: Compensation and integration. *Harvard Education Review 38*(1), 100–115.

Community Education Partners. (2004). *Community Education Partners: Our Program: Raising the Bar.* Houston, TX: author. Retrieved June 15, 2005, from www.communityeducationpartners.com/program.asp.

Dewey, J. (1916). *Democracy and Education*. Allendale, SC: Macmillan and Company.

Frug, J. (1998). City services. *New York University Law Review 73*(1), (April, 1998), 23–96.

Goss v. Lopez. (1975). 419 U.S. 565, 95 S. Ct. 729.

Harvard University Advancement Projects and Civil Rights Project. (2000). *Opportunities Suspended: The Devastating Consequences of Zero Tolerance and School Discipline*. Retrieved March 23, 2004, from www.civilrightsproject.harvard.edu/research/disci pline/opport_suspended.php.

Houston Independent School District. (2004). *HISD Connect: School Profile: Community Education Partners*. Retrieved June 15, 2005, from www.http://dept.houstonisd.org/ profiles/CEP_SE.

Irvine, J. J. (1991). *Black Students and School Failure: Policies, Practices, and Prescriptions*. Westport, CT: Greenwood Press.

Kerka, S. (2003). *Alternatives for At-Risk and Out-of-School Youth* (Report No. EDO-CE-03-248). Washington, DC: Office of Educational Research and Improvement (ERIC Document Reproduction Service No. ED 482 327).

Kleiner, B., Porch, R., and Farris, E. (2002). *Public Alternative Schools and Programs for Students at Risk of Education Failure: 2000–01* (NCES 2000–004). U.S. Department of Education, OERI. Washington, DC: U.S. Department of Education, National Center for Educational Statistics (NCES).

Lehr, C. A., and Lange, C. M. (2003). Alternative schools and the students they serve: Perceptions of state directors of special education. *Policy Research Brief 14*(2), University of Minnesota, Minneapolis, Institute on Community Research.

Lehr, C. A., Lanners, F. J., and Lange, C. M. (2003). Alternative schools: Policy and legislation across the United States. *Policy Research Brief* 14(1), University of Minnesota, Minneapolis, Institute on Community Research.

Levin, H. (1975). Some methodological problems in economic policy research: Determining how much should be spent on compensatory education. *Education and Urban Society 7*(3), 303–333.

McCarthy, M. M., Cambron-McCabe, N. H., and Thomas, S. B. (2004). *Legal Rights of Teachers and Students*. Boston, MA: Allyn and Bacon.

McGee, J. (2001). Reflections of an alternative school administrator. *Phi Delta Kappan 82*(8), 588–592.

Mississippi State Department of Education. (2001). *Alternative Education Handbook* (Report No. EC 309 151). Jackson, MS: Mississippi State Department of Education (ERIC Document Reproduction Service No. 468 668).

Nevares v. San Marcos C.I.S.D., 111F3d 25 (5th Cir. 1997).

North Carolina Education and Law Project. (1997). *Alternative Schools: Short-Term Solution with Long-Term Consequences*. Raleigh, NC: Author.

Orfield, G. (2004). *Dropouts in America*. Cambridge, MA: Harvard Education Press.

Pollock, M. (2004). *Colormute: Race Talk Dilemmas in an American School*. Princeton, NJ: Princeton University Press.

Raywid, M. A. (1994). Alternative schools: The state of the art. *Educational Leadership 52*(1), 26–31.

Reyes, A. H. (2001). Alternative education: The criminalization of student behavior. *Fordham Urban Law Journal 29*(2), 539–559.

Reyes, A. (2003, May). Alternative schools: Analysis of student enrollment in Texas alternative schools. Paper presented at the Harvard Civil Rights Meeting on School to Prison Pipeline, Cambridge, MA.

Reyes, A. (April 12–16, 2004). *Leaders in Schools with High Hispanic Enrollments*. San Diego, CA: American Association for Educational Research.

Rimer, S. (2004, January 4). Some unruly students now face arrest, not detention. *The New York Times*, pp. A1, A15.

Rosenberg, I. (2003). Random suspicionless drug testing: Are students no longer afforded fourth amendment protection? *New York Law Review 4, 46*(3–4), 821–849.

Texas Criminal Code. (2000). Texas Code of Criminal Procedure Article 15.27 (a).

Texas Education Agency. (1998). Texas Administrators' Code, TAC 75.164. Austin, TX: Author.

Texas Education Agency. (2002). *Alternative Education Accountability System Manual*. Austin, TX: Author.

Texas Education Agency. (2002). *Comprehensive Annual Report on Texas Public Schools: A Report to the 78th Texas Legislature*, p. 45. Austin, TX: Author.

Texas Education Agency. (2003). *Texas 2002 Comprehensive Annual Report on Texas Public Schools*. Austin, TX: Author.

Texas Education Agency. (2004). *Alternative Education Accountability System Manual*. Austin, TX: Author.

Texas Education Agency. (2005). Texas education agency adequate yearly progress evaluations. Retrieved August 11, 2005, from www.tea.state.tx.us/ayp.

Texas Education Agency. (2005, February). *Texas 2004 Comprehensive Annual Report on Texas Public Schools*. Austin, TX: Author.

Texas Education Agency. (2005, March). *Enrollment in Texas Public Schools 2003–2004*. Austin, TX: Author.

Texas Education Code Annotated. *Subtitle G, Safe Schools, Chapter 37 Discipline Law and Order*. Vernon Supp. (2002).

Texas Education Code Annotated. §29.089. Vernon Supp. (2002).

Texas Education Code Annotated. §37.000. Vernon Supp. (2002).

Texas Education Code Annotated. §37.001. Vernon Supp. (2002).

Texas Education Code Annotated. §37.006. Vernon Supp. (2002).

Texas Education Code Annotated. §37.006(a). Vernon Supp. (2002).

Texas Education Code Annotated. §37.007. Vernon Supp. (2002).

Texas Education Code Annotated. §37.007(a)(d)(e). Vernon Supp. (2002).

Texas Education Code Annotated. §37.007(a)(2)(3). Vernon Supp. (2002).

Texas Education Code Annotated. §37.006(d). Vernon Supp. (2002).

Texas Education Code Annotated. Chapter 37, 2001. Vernon Supp. (2002).

Texas Education Code Annotated. §37.008–37.0011. Vernon Supp. (2002).

Texas Juvenile Probation Commission and Texas Education Agency. (2002). *Juvenile Justice Alternative Education Programs Performance Assessment Report*. Austin, TX: Author.

Texas Penal Code. §37.007(a)(1). Vernon Supp. (2002).

Tobin, T., and Sprague, J. (2000). Alternative education strategies: Reducing violence in school and community. *Journal of Emotional and Behavioral Disorders 8*(3), 177–187.

Valencia, R. R. (1997). *The Evolution of Deficit Thinking*. Washington, DC: The Falmer Press.

Verdugo, R. R. (2002). Race-ethnicity, social class, and zero tolerance policies: The cultural and structural wars. *Education and Urban Society* 35(1), 50–75.

Young, T. (1990). *Public Alternative Education*. New York: Teachers College Press.

Young, T. (1992). *Guidelines for Alternative Programs: A Guide to the Education and Training of Youth in At-Risk Situations*. Austin, TX: Texas Dropout Information Clearinghouse.

4

The Courtroom Drama: Criminal Certification of Student Behavior

Imagine that you are an eleventh grade student. Your mother suffers from migraine headaches. The doctor has periodically hospitalized your mother. Your father is also in poor health but has steady employment in a local steel factory. Last night was a particularly bad night for your mother. She had painful headaches and did not sleep all night. You did not get much sleep yourself, but in the morning, you made the decision to go to school. While you were in class, you fell asleep. The teacher asks another student to wake you. Upon being awakened, you pushed and cursed at the student assigned to wake you. You are sent to the principal's office, where the school police, who is also a peace officer, charges you with "disruption of school." You are given a ticket and told that the local justice of the peace will notify you of a court date for you to appear in court to defend yourself.

On the day that you are to appear in court, your mother is suffering from migraine headaches. Your mother writes a letter to the judge requesting a postponement. Your mother explains to the judge that her health caused her to be on disability. The court date is rescheduled; however, it had to be rescheduled a second time because both your parents were in the hospital. Finally, when your mother is able to find someone to drive her to court, she did not have the money to pay forty-eight dollars for the court fees. She explains to the judge that the family was completely out of money. It seems that after bills, they only have twenty-five dollars for all other expenses. Your mother promises the judge she will pay as soon as the family has the money. She explains to the judge that she thinks her husband will get a promotion at the steel factory and then they will have more money.

71

The judge suspects that you may also have a disability. She requests that you be evaluated for learning disabilities. A few weeks later, the judge is notified that the evaluation reveals that you have ADHD. This entire process is played out in court. The school is never involved. The school's involvement started and ended when the student was given a ticket and charged with "disruption of school," a class C misdemeanor in accordance with state zero tolerance policies.

In a second situation, imagine that you are an eleven-year-old student who is considered smaller than the other sixth-grade, middle-school students. Sometimes you have to be a "tough" guy to show that you are like your peers. You are angry about the divorce between your mother and father. Your mother has custody of you, but you want to live with your father, who you miss. As a kid who is small for your age, you have to play tough to get through some school challenges. One day, you are horse playing with a friend who says, "Don't touch me!" You rise to the challenge and touch the other student, which leads to a school hallway fight.

You are sent to the assistant principal's office, where a peace officer gives you a ticket for "disorderly conduct fighting," a class C misdemeanor. This is your second offense. In front of the judge, your parent (a single mom) informs the judge that this is your second fight. "Jimmy is acting out because he wants to go live with his father." You are an undersized eleven-year-old kid caught in the middle of a divorce that you do not understand. All you know is that you miss your father. All you want to do is be back with your father so that life can be the way it was before the divorce. The judge asks your mother, "Where does the father stand on this matter?" Your mother confirms that you will be moving in with your father and will be going to a new school. The judge gives you a ninety-day suspension of sentence and deferral of final disposition. In ninety days, you should return to court with your mother. The social worker recommends that you be reevaluated when you return in ninety days. The judge orders that, when you return, your father and your mother must return with you.

All of this occurs without the school's involvement. In retrospect, this student is having a difficult time adjusting to the loss of a parent. There is a lot going on in his life that requires family counseling to help the student understand the trauma his family is experiencing. Giving Jimmy a ticket and sending him to court only makes matters worse. The child acts out and gets what he wants; however, he must disrupt his education. While the ticket was meant as a punishment for the student's behavior, in reality it is the reward he wanted. Now that he is in trouble, he gets to go live with his father. He has achieved his goal. One can only hope that the arrangement with Dad is going to work; otherwise, there will be one more child out there in transition from one school to another and from Mom to Dad and back to Mom. In this case, neither behavior nor discipline is positively affected; however, the school was able to efficiently remove the problem from the school without disrupting the education of those students who were in school to learn.

In a third case, imagine that you are the child of a parent who moved from Mexico to the United States looking for work. You would rather stay in Mexico with your friends, but you had no choice in the matter. You come to the United States with your parents. When you enter school in the United States, you become an excellent student. Academically, you are doing so well that you become a favorite among your teachers. Your middle school imposes a new rule. All students must wear a school uniform. Your parents cannot afford a new uniform. You miss school for ten days because you do not have the required uniform. The school sends a notice to your home citing your parents because you are absent from school. You are chaarged with a Class C misdemeanor (Texas Education Code §25.094(e), 2004). You and one of your parents must show up at the local Justice of the Peace Court to defend yourself and to pay your fine.

On the assigned day, you and your mother show up in court to defend your crime. The judge becomes concerned when she reviews your case. It seems that several of your teachers have written telling her what a wonderful student you are. They plead with her not to fine you with the crime charged. The judge cannot understand why such an outstanding citizen is in her court. Upon inquiring from your mother, the judge is informed that the family simply does not have the money to buy the uniform the school requires. The judge shares your situation with a group of business women, and they volunteer to purchase some uniforms. In this case the school required all students to wear uniforms without realizing some students may not have the money to buy uniforms in spite of the high number of low-income students enrolled in the school. When the student was absent from school for ten days because the family did not have the money to purchase the proper uniform, the school issued the student a ticket for a class C misdemeanor. The parents were also cited for a Class C misdemeanor offense of "parents contributing to non attendance" (Texas Education Code §25.093(a) (c), 2004, p. 154). Parents may be fined up to $500. The fines are divided between the court and the school district (Downing, 2005). The uniform problem was efficiently handled by transferring the problem out of the school and into the judicial system. There was no involvement from a school counselor, a social worker, or even a teacher aide.

Imagine that you are a high school student who is assaulted by the school bullies. You are sent to the office and given a ticket for "disorderly conduct of fighting," a class C misdemeanor. You are given a ticket for being "involved in the disorderly conduct of fighting." The bullies who assaulted you do not receive a ticket. You show up in court with your mother as the law requires. The judge reviews the case and, in court, inquires on the where-abouts of the other parties. She is informed that you are the only person charged. In this case, school administrators used their discretion as to whom to charge. Upon the judge's insistence, the other parties are also charged and appear in court.

Imagine that you are an eighteen-year-old kid who wants to impress your peers. You bring a bottle of juice to school. Somehow the rumor gets started that the juice is spiked. The juice bottle gets passed around as if it were spiked. The assistant principal rounds up all the suspects; however, after checking the contents of the juice bottle, it is concluded that it is not spiked. You get a ticket for the "disruption of classes." Once you appear before the Justice of the Peace (JP) judge, she assigns you to eighteen hours of commu-nity service, and you are required to attend a clinic on alcoholism. The case is dismissed once you have completed your community service and the six months of deferred disposition.

These cases represent the dramas played out in front of a Justice of the Peace Court in Texas, but it could be in Ohio (Rimer, 2004). Zero tolerance policies in Texas and many other states have changed the image of the Justice of the Peace Court, county courts, and municipal courts. The traditional image of a Justice of the Peace Court is one of two lovers knocking on the door of the local JP to ask the judge to perform a marriage. The judge pulls out his Bible and forms for the marriage license. The JP's wife serves as the witness and the organ player. The class C misdemeanor stories cited in this chapter are true dramas of courtroom observations in a Texas county. The court ruled on traffic violations in the morning and student class C misde-meanor offenses in the afternoon. The afternoon was reserved for hearing stu-dent zero tolerance violations from approximately three local high schools.

Around twelve o'clock in the afternoon students and parents start to gather outside the courtroom. Many parents and students approach a small window where a clerk, who normally collects partial or full payments, cash, credit cards, or debit cards for court costs and fines for traffic or other violations, tells inquiring students and parents, "If you'll just step into the courtroom, court will start at 1:30 p.m." The hallway is filled with the seventy defendants and a minimum of one parent per student. In some cases, two parents are present. In some rare cases, students are accompanied by a parent and an attorney.

Much happened to prepare the stage for the drama of the Justice of the Peace student behavior court hearings. While in school, each defendant as a public school student was given a ticket by the school peace officer or a county constable for conduct according to state zero tolerance policy. The court receives the student tickets for class C misdemeanors and notifies parents, managing conservator, or guardian of the individual charged by issuing a summons (Vernon's Ann. Texas C.C.P. Art. 45.057, 2005).

While there are three judicial jurisdictions that hear cases generated by zero tolerance policy, the Justice of the Peace Court hears the most minor offenses, class C misdemeanors (TEC §37.104, 2004). There are sixteen JP courts that follow a similar routine in the county. The JP court hears 140 school behavior cases two days a week for ten months of the year and reserves a second day for school attendance cases. The judge has instituted Saturday court for many of the parents who have no transportation to get to court during the week. According to the judge, most of the cases she hears are for classroom disruption and disorderly conduct for language used in the classroom. There are some drug cases. They are mostly for kids who are selling their parents' or their own prescription drugs, like depression medicine or mood blockers. Some students are charged with selling and distributing over-the-counter drugs, like corycidum pills. The more serious drug cases are heard in state or county juvenile court. The most serious cases the judge hears are for fighting and students making threats.

In courtroom observations, it was noted that in almost 25 percent of the cases heard, students commented to the judge that they would be transferring from the school that gave them the ticket. Transferring out of the student's home school may seem like a win-win situation for everyone. The student may feel that by transferring out of the home school, they will have the opportunity to start over. The parent may feel that by transferring out of the school, they can transfer out of the court's jurisdiction. The school wins because state policy allows the accountability scores of a student who transfers during the school year to be attributed to the school district and not to any school. They will be calculated in the district averages (Texas Education Agency, 2004). In reality, transferring out of one's home school disrupts the student's education. They leave their classes in the middle of the semester. The new teacher in the receiving school may not feel responsible for helping the student catch up with her class. Transferring may lead to a student falling farther behind and eventually dropping out of school (Opportunities Suspended, 2000; Rumbaut, 2005).

The courtroom drama continues as one student after another approaches the judge's bench. As the judge has predicted, the common themes that run through each drama are fighting and foul language. Students explain that they did not "like" the other student involved in the fight. Two students were involved in a fight after an Internet posting about sexually transmitted diseases. There is always the student who walks up to another student in a "threatening way" or who looks at the student in a threatening way. There is the student who did not strike the first blow and only fought to protect herself. The leading characters in the abusive-language cases explained to the judge that they did not mean to say "shit and damn" or to say to another student, "Bitch, I'm going to kick your ass."

In order for the court to complete the daily docket, each case must be heard in three minutes. In those three minutes, the judge must ask questions that she has formulated from previously reading the case folders. The novice district attorney provided by the county must be satisfied that the case is properly prosecuted. The social worker assigned to the court by the county children's services must ensure that the welfare of the young defendant is protected. She must also provide support to the young defendant and the family in context of declining social services available to defendants. For example, finding a slot in a drug rehabilitation program may take several weeks, if they are even available. For every case that stands in front of the judge, she attempts to provide counseling, saying, "If someone walks up to you in a threatening way, you need to pull away to avoid a fight." She probes defendants and their parents to get answers to her questions. In most cases, the judge will give the defendants a ninety-day suspension of sentence and deferral of final disposition. She may also assign them to counseling, conflict resolution, anger management workshops, substance abuse, and other workshops; however, the student is also assigned to workshops which can charge thirty to fifty dollars. For students who are charged with "shooting the finger," she will assign a class in sign language. She will request student assessments for suspicious cases. The judge may also assess a fine ranging from one to five hundred dollars. Every case is assessed court costs ranging from forty-eight to sixty-eight dollars. While all students are entitled to a trial by jury, less than 1 percent will request one.

The judge must follow up on defendants who failed to appear (FTA) in court. If a student is seventeen years of age and older, the court may issue a continuing obligation to appear. Then she will issue an arrest warrant. If the student is younger than seventeen years of age, she will issue and order the Department of Public Safety to suspend the defendent's driver's license or permit, or deny the issuance of a license or permit until the court order is compiled.

Zero tolerance policy neither gives consideration to circumstances nor allows for administrative discretion; consequently, in short plays like the drama of Condalisa Nice, honor students find themselves in court for the first discipline infraction in a lifetime of academic achievement. Condalisa Nice, an African American female, was charged with "disorderly conduct fighting." Condalisa pleaded guilty and the judge gave her a ninety-day suspension of sentence and deferral of final disposition. She explains that she and a friend were walking down the hallway having a conversation that escalated into an argument with one student pushing the other. Condalisa has a 4.95 GPA. She is in the top 15 percent of her class in a large, suburban high school. The assistant principal explained to the parent that if she had any discretion in the punishment she would take into consideration Condalisa's academic record and her unblemished record of behavior; however, zero tolerance policies were mandatory.

The "one strike and you are out" policy may have a long-term affect on an otherwise promising career. Will Condalisa walk out of the courtroom, complete her assigned workshop, turn eighteen, petition the court to expunge her record, and go to college? Will Condalisa's self-esteem be so affected by the fact that she was given a ticket for a class C misdemeanor that she will live up to lower expectations? Will Condalisa continue to excel in school and graduate before she turns eighteen, only to be told that she has been disqualified for all scholarships because she has a criminal record? If Condolisa goes to law school, she must disclose her class C misdemeanor.

A third theme heard during the JP hearings was trespassing on school grounds. According to state zero tolerance policy, trespassing on school grounds is a class C misdemeanor (TEC §37.107, 2004). The school policy is that if you are a student on that campus, you cannot return to the school after your last class. One student explains that he returned to school to retrieve a book; however, when he did not respond to the security guard's warning, he was cited for trespassing.

The cases cited may seem fictional, but sadly, they are real-life dramas. While these cases appeared in a public judicial system in Texas, they are appearing on a regular basis all over the country (Rimer, 2004). Using tickets for school disruption is the magic pill—the catchall cure for adolescent misbehavior. While no doctor would prescribe the same pill for migraines, diabetes, the flu, a cold, high blood pressure, or measles, schools are willing to use tickets charging students with criminal infractions for family health and social issues, for disability, for being too poor to buy school uniforms, or for being an innocent kid who was the victim of bullying.

Neither pills nor court can replace adult supervision for behavioral issues that require ongoing, regular adult guidance to acquire knowledge, reason, and wisdom. Comer (2001) describes the link between a child's learning and development as a process with the more mature caretaker helping the less mature to channel potentially harmful aggressive energy into energy of constructive learning, work, and play. The more mature stages of development continue to build on the past and are continuously mediated by more mature people (Comer, 2001). All children, but particularly minority children, are dependent on willing, mature caretakers who are capable of guiding their maturity and development.

The student behavior drama of the Justice of the Peace courtroom exemplifies the need for schools to realize that children and teenagers mature cognitively and emotionally through their life experiences, education, and guidance from adults. The research that adolescents do not acquire knowledge, reason, and wisdom without trial and tribulation applies in many of the cases heard in the JP court. Historically, the role of teachers and other adults has been to aid children in their growth and through the difficult period of adolescence by providing expectations and by providing constructive feedback. Adults provide reasonable responses to undesirable behavior. Adults help students develop responsible behavior, better problem-solving skills, and better social skills. The research shows the importance of the need for children to develop strong, trusting relationships with key adults (Harvard, 2000). Get tough school discipline policies do not provide opportunities for adults to guide student behavior. They are designed to remove adult discretion from the student discipline process. They provide supervising teachers and administrators with specific and efficient rules for removing the student and the student's problems out of the schoolhouse and into the courthouse, as in the Justice of the Peace drama.

In the defense of teachers, there is also the reality that they are not rewarded for promoting student development, for developing good citizens, for solving student's social problems, for communicating with parents to bridge home and school, or for working with communities to resolve student drug issues. Teachers are rewarded for improving student achievement on state accountability standards. If they are successful, they are rewarded with extra income based on their school accountability rating. If they do not succeed, they become the target of the central office for improving classroom instruction; consequently, some teachers have banded together to protect classroom instructional time and maximize instructional time. According to one report, 97 percent of teachers say good student discipline is a prerequisite for a successful school (Johnson, 2004). Teachers believe that they could teach more effectively if they did not have to spend so much time with disruptive students (Johnson, 2004).

Admittedly, teachers and parents are capable of nurturing student behavior. New teachers are a different breed. Many come from the average American family of 1.2 children. They have rarely been responsible for children as siblings or even baby-sitting. Older teachers came from larger families and had lifetime responsibilities for younger siblings or earned spending money by baby-sitting. For new teachers, student discipline must be learned using behavioral management techniques provided by some teacher preparation

programs or ongoing staff development. Some parents are equally as ill prepared; consequently, there are some students who know how to manipulate
parents. For example, in the case of the eleven-year-old who was in court for
fighting in school, what he really wanted was to get in trouble so that he could
go live with his father. No one stood up to this eleven-year-old. The school
gave him two tickets, and the mother turned him over to his father.

Maximizing instructional time means that student social, economic, language, and cultural problems be moved out of the classroom to allow efficient
use of instructional time. In the 1990s, when accountability testing became
prominent, Texas minority policy makers believed that quality of instruction
for minority students was so poor that testing could provide a measure of
accountability for holding teachers in high-poverty, high-minority schools
more responsible for their instruction (Dubose, 1998). Texas policy makers
were concerned about the extremely poor performance of the inner-city public schools that constituents are forced to attend (Dubose, 1998). Texas
minority state legislators expressed concerns that the low student performance meant writing "off a generation of children while we're fighting to
improve the horrible public schools they're forced to attend" (Dubose, 1998).
It was in that context that minority policy makers supported accountability.
Accountability may only measure minimum basic skills, but at a minimum,
it assures that minority students will have minimum skills as opposed to no
skills. Accountability was never intended to supercede student development.

CLASS C MISDEMEANORS

While class C misdemeanors are the lowest level of juvenile crimes that may
be expunged, they are nonetheless a crime. Every class C misdemeanor is
assigned an identification number in the Justice Information Management
System along with all other crimes committed in the state. The system expo-
ses kids to the criminal system at a very young age. Every judge is required
to give parents and students information on how to expunge a juvenile record.
When the student completes the sentence prescribed by the judge, the case is
dismissed. Once the student turns eighteen years of age, they may petition
the court to have their case expunged; however, according to one judge, 75
percent of her cases will be expunged. A less-sophisticated 25 percent of
juvenile defendants will keep their juvenile records for failure to complete
deferred prosecution and failure to notify the court of completion of judg-
ment (interview conducted December 4, 2004, with Judge Delgado).

Overage students will not be eligible to expunge juvenile student crime
records. There are cases of overage students who do not have the same option

offered to minors. One alternative education program reported that in the sixth grade, 24 percent of their students were fourteen years old. In the tenth grade, 13 percent of their students were eighteen years old and 1 percent was nineteen years old. In the eleventh grade, 10 percent were nineteen years old and 3 percent were twenty years old (Students Overage by Grade Level, 2003–2004). These data support the research on overage students in the public schools who will be subjected to the disadvantage of having a criminal record before they can graduate from high school.

The second problem with relying on class C misdemeanor infractions for student discipline is the subjective language of what constitutes a class C misdemeanor. There are three class C misdemeanors in the Texas zero policies. Class C misdemeanors include disruption of classes, disruption of transportation, and trespassing on school grounds (37.107, 37.124, 37.126). Disruption of transportation and trespassing on school grounds provide very specific and direct language; however, the language for disruption of classes is very subjective.

According to the Texas Education Code, Section 37.124, disruption of class is defined as follows: "A person commits an offense if the person on school property or on public property within 500 feet of school property, alone or in concert with others intentionally disrupts the conduct of class or other school activities." The policy extends the definition of disruption to include "disrupting the conduct of classes or other social activities." Disrupting the conduct of classes or other social activities may include "emitting noise of an intensity that prevents or hinders classroom instruction." Without a clear definition, "emitting noise of intensity that prevents or hinders classroom instruction" may include a loud sneeze that catches the teacher's attention. It may also include a student dropping a book or any other strange noises that teenagers make. Definitions for "enticing or attempting to entice a student away from a class or other school activity that the student is required to attend" may appear simple and clear. Generally, the assumption is that one student is tempting another student to skip class, but who is cited for the class C misdemeanor? Is it the innocent student who has no intention of skipping class but is caught in the hallway with a student who really wants another student to convince him not to skip class? Zero tolerance policies do not allow for consideration of circumstances; consequently, there is a trend for punishing innocent students.

Another infraction that is classified as a class C misdemeanor includes "preventing or attempting to prevent a student from attending a class or other school activity that the student is required to attend. Entering the classroom without the consent of either the principal, or the teacher" presents another reason to ticket students. A student commits a class C misdemeanor if through either acts of misconduct or the use of loud or profane language the student disrupts class activities. This would apply to the case of the student who fell asleep in class and used loud and profane language when he was awakened by another student. The policy on class C misdemeanors can be subject to the interpretation of numerous teachers and school administrators. In addition to class C misdemeanors, zero tolerance policies mandate more serious offenses like class A and class B misdemeanor cases. Class C misdemeanor cases are heard in the Justice of the Peace Court and the Municipal Teen Court. Class A and class B misdemeanor cases are heard in the county juvenile district court.

There are no data for the number of student tickets issued in school and charging students with class A, B, or C misdemeanors. This chapter only discusses class C misdemeanor as the most common offense. Since students are charged in county or municipal courts, the state education agency is not required to report the data. In most cases, a student will receive a ticket and short-term, campus-based discipline. For example, in the case of a student who receives a ticket for "minor in possession" (MIP), the students will be allowed to stay in school but may receive three days in the school detention center. If the student receives a ticket and is also placed in detention, suspension, expulsion, or DAEP, the state public education information system (PEIMS) will report the data in the appropriate category; however, it is unlikely they will be suspended, expelled, or placed in a DAEP for the class C misdemeanor. Suspension is reserved for the more serious offenses, like assault or possession of marijuana or alcohol. Expulsions are reserved for felony offenses like weapons or drugs; consequently, the state education agency does not track student class C misdemeanors.

There are some data available from the judicial system. For example, the workload aggregate data for Justice of the Peace Courts in one large urban county in Texas showed that, in 2004, the JP courts alone heard 34,553 education class C misdemeanor cases. Texas school policy mandated the use of student tickets for student discipline behavior in 1995. According to "The Justice of the Peace Courts," a report on the Texas courts, for the period between 1996 and 2004, the number of new JP cases increased every year since 1996 and in 2004 exceeded three million cases for the first time (State of Texas Judicial Report, 2004). According to the state report, in 2003–2004, the JP courts heard 60,791 failures to attend school cases and 41,378 parents contributing to nonschool attendance. During the same period, the JP courts issued 704,895 arrest warrants for failure to attend court for class C misdemeanors. While these state data may include class C misdemeanor cases other than education cases, all education cases heard by the JP court are for class C misdemeanor or attendance. The state data only report class C misdemeanor cases in the JP court. In every county jurisdiction, there are three courts that hear zero tolerance cases: the JP court, the municipal court, and the county juvenile district court. Data from one jurisdiction alone report 34,553 education-related cases for one year and raise concerns that students are exposed to the criminal system at a very young age.

MUNICIPAL TEEN COURT

In addition to county Justice of the Peace Courts, Municipal Teen Courts have been set up to hear the mounting number of class C misdemeanor cases for large, urban school districts and municipal juvenile curfew restrictions. Public observations of teen court hearings and interviews with the judge provided an insight into the cases heard by the Municipal Teen Court judge. Observations of the proceedings showed a courtroom with space for about 100 students and their parents. The defendants were almost entirely Latino and Spanish speaking. The judge confirmed that it was a requirement that he be Spanish speaking in order to hear the cases. The judge commented, "Lately, I've been getting a lot of cases for 'not following school instructions.'" Teen court serves juveniles under the age of seventeen. They must appear with a parent or a guardian. They may bring a lawyer; however, this is rarely done. The more affluent students are able to bring a lawyer with them. The advantage is that most lawyers know the judge and the district attorney's representatives through professional activities, which speeds up the process in favor of the student defendant.

The procedures for teen court include arraignment, pretrial, or trial by jury. If they plead "not guilty," they will be given a trial date. In most cases, the defendants plead guilty to the charge. Less than 1 percent request a trial by jury. The judge will fine the student from one to five hundred dollars. The judge will set the terms and conditions of the probation that must be followed for a period of up to six months. The case will be reset, and if the student successfully completes the terms and conditions of the probation, the case will be dismissed. There will be no record of a conviction. Probation allows you to receive a second chance.

When the student enters a plea of guilty or no contest, they may request community service hours in lieu of paying a fine. The judge may assign the case to a teen community service program in lieu of paying a fine. The student may be required to attend a workshop. Failure to Appear (FTA) in court will trigger issuance of an arrest warrant for the student who is eighteen years old. The municipal teen court hears class C misdemeanor cases for zero tolerance policies, including tickets for school activities, alcohol and tobacco, failure to attend school, and other school violations. They also hear teen cases for violations of city ordinances like teen curfew.

Teen court observations revealed a train of parents and students appearing before the judge to plead no contest to the class C misdemeanor cases. One case that approached the judge was the case of a student charged with fighting in the classroom. Ironically, the student was assigned to a school that was testing a school reform program focused on a learning model grounded on collaboration. According to the facts, eight students were collaborating on a student learning project when a fight broke out in the work group. In the interest of time, all eight students were given a ticket and sent to court for the judge to resolve the conflict.

According to the judge, many of the cases he hears are "school stuff. These are school discipline things that when I went to school, the teacher settled." In many cases, the judge observed that functional illiteracy is a greater issue than discipline. "Many of the students I see here are functionally illiterate. They don't tell you that they can't read. I just sense that. When they can't read the waiver that you ask them to sign, you know they can't read." The judge explained that it was necessary for him to speak Spanish. "I have to use my neighborhood Spanish to sit in this court. Many of my students are English-as-second-language students. I would say that 80 percent of my cases are Spanish-speaking students who can't read."

Like the Justice of the Peace judge, the teen court judge attempted to help his defendants by referring them to social services; however, social service resources have been depleted, limiting his ability to assist defendants in need. He provided the case of a couple who came to his court in response to a student ticket. These parents came to the court seeking help to find their runaway child. He could not help the couple, however, because there are no programs to which he could refer them. The judge described this case as one of his hard-core cases. These were the cases of kids who ran away or who were doing drugs. "Five years ago, my listing of referral programs was five inches wide. Today, there are fewer than fifty programs in the entire county. I remember the case of the local cheerleader who was a habitual runaway. The parents came to court in response to a ticket for a Class C misdemeanor offense of "parents contributing to non attendance" (TEC §25.093(a) (c), 2004, p. 154). I find myself giving parents like this advice on how to file a missing persons report. The young cheerleader was eventually found dead. For the real hard-core cases, there are no programs to help them."

CONCLUSIONS

The cases reviewed in this chapter were real cases publicly observed in a Justice of the Peace and a municipal court that are responsible for prosecuting class C misdemeanor cases generated by state zero tolerance policies. While students sixteen years of age and younger will be able to petition the court to expunge their records, 25 percent will never petition the court. The several overage seventeen- to twenty-one-year-olds who are charged with class C misdemeanors do not have the privilege to petition the court and will carry a criminal record for school discipline offenses. Students who do not show up for court may lose their privilege to have a driver's license, or they may have an arrest warrant issued. The law is very clear on what a student must do once they have received a discipline class C misdemeanor ticket, but what are the consequences of exposing students at such a young age to the criminal system? Rather than preparing productive responsible citizens, the system is flowing students out of our schools and into our prisons (Wald and Losen, 2003).

By using one response for all student behavioral cases without consideration to circumstances, the policy has redefined the historical responsibilities that adults have for providing guidance for student development. Who will guide the development of tomorrow's citizens? What are the consequences? The search for school safety produces collateral damage. Innocent students are prosecuted. Students may also be subjected to double jeopardy in cases where students are given a citation and also assigned to campus short-term detention. Student social, health, immigrant, linguistic, cultural, and economic problems are transferred to the courtroom. Teachers are overextended on improving test scores and do not have time to develop student/teacher relationships. Teachers do not have the time to provide adult guidance that young people need to develop into productive citizens. In some cases, teachers no longer have the time to regularly communicate with parents.

The message from zero tolerance policies that criminalizes school disruptions is that sociological and psychological issues should not be a consideration in education. Hard-core criminal behavior and drug problems are treated the same as being too poor to buy a school uniform or being too poor to afford health care. Students get mixed messages when punishments become rewards or when punishment is equally dispersed regardless of the offense. In the end, there are no services for desperate parents who are looking for a runaway, other than a ticket from the school for nonschool attendance.

How will ticketing identify, assess, and redirect a really violent student? For example, one teacher identified a student who she believed to be really disturbed when he was in her class. She observed the student continuously provoking other children in ways that were indicative of his rage. One day, the student calmly got up out of his desk, unlatched the pencil shavings from the wall-mount pencil sharpener, and dumped them all over another child's head. He stained the child's clothes and shamed him in front of his peers

(Cocina, 2004). For this disturbed student, fights, arguments, gross profanity, insults (with teachers and students), and disruption were daily occurrences. The student was never removed from the classroom or assessed for other problems. These students fall between the cracks, becoming more dangerous; however, the reality is that there are fewer and fewer school-related or other community services for potentially unstable and disturbed students.

The most dramatic change that emerges from zero tolerance policies is the transfer of basic adolescent behavior development from the school house to the courthouse and the formal disengagement of teachers in their student supervising role. There were several cases prosecuted in the court drama that before 1995 were settled by teachers and administrators. For example, there was the case of the student who shared a bottle of juice that was rumored to be spiked. While the prank caused class disruptions, this prank has played itself out in U.S. schools for at least for fifty years; however, in the past, adults supervising students in school had time to talk with students about what is appropriate behavior. Like student pranks, fighting has been a school discipline problem since schools were opened in the United States. In some country school houses, in order to keep his job, the teacher had to be big enough to fight off the biggest student in the school (Tyack, 1974). Will students pay their court fees, complete the required anger management workshop, and never fight again? Is there a difference between a workshop and the care that a teacher shows for a student by counseling them and helping them to understand the virtues of getting along with peers? There is a significant difference, and young people know the difference.

A major concern with ticketing students for behavior is that all crimes are treated with the same pill. A student abusing drugs is equated with a student who sleeps in class because his mother is so ill that she keeps him awake at night. Drugs present serious problems that need the attention of the school and the community. If students are going to school and selling drugs that they buy at Safeway, Walgreen's, Wal-Mart, CVS, or some other neighborhood store, sending a student to a drug workshop is not enough. Schools, communities, and businesses need to take the initiative to solve serious drug problems as a community. If students are selling their drugs or their parents' drugs to other students, parents need be involved in solving this problem. Schools need to make real efforts to solve student behavior problems. Punishment alone does not solve the problem.

The difference between the role that teachers and principals supervising students ten to fifteen years ago played and the role they play today is that the students and society have changed. Ideologically, students are not buying what schools are selling for discipline. Students are more outspoken and knowledgeable of student rights. Teachers and administrators have to earn the respect of today's youth. Today, race is an issue. Demographically, student populations are different from the teachers teaching them. Almost 45 percent of the students in U.S. schools are minority, and 80 percent of the teachers are white. In the municipal court, 80 percent of the cases heard were from immigrant students who could not read in English and could only converse with the judge in Spanish. This poses an instructional issue that is the responsibility of teachers and principals. Giving nonliterate immigrants tickets for classroom disruption poses ethical and legal questions. These students are more likely to do poorly on school accountability tests that they are required to take after up to three years in a Texas public school (TEC §39.0231, 2004). Punishment for misbehavior does not address the problem of literacy.

The differences between student populations and teacher resources matter in supervising student development and student behavior. The mismatch of race, class, and social backgrounds between teachers and students can create conflicts in a process that requires engaging relationships. Group relations are more harmonious in homogeneous relations. The data show that school populations are very heterogeneous and diverse. Teachers require intensive staff development to acquire the knowledge, skills, and dispositions needed to discipline and guide students in diverse student environments. The patterns of students who were charged with class C misdemeanors showed a disproportionate number were minority students. One judge commented that 80 percent of the cases for which he was responsible were immigrant students who did not speak English and were nonliterate in English. Race is an issue for class C misdemeanor offenses.

None of the discipline issues brought to court are simple issues to solve; merely moving them from one theater to another, however, will not solve the problems that kids bring to school. One can only wonder what kind of citizens this "strike one and you are out" system will produce. On the other hand, just as teachers have been rewarded for improving accountability scores in their school, they should also be rewarded for improving behavior, for working with the community, and for working with parents. The teacher reward system only rewards test scores.

REFERENCES

Ayers, W., Dohrn, B., and Ayers, R., eds. (2001). *Zero Tolerance: Resisting the Drive for Punishment in Our Schools*. New York: New Press.

Cocina, E. (2004). A term paper presented to Dr. Joy Phillips at the University of Houston, Fall 2004.

Comer, J. (2001, April 23). Schools that develop children. *The American Prospect 12*(7). Retrieved July 20, 2005, from www.prospect.org/print/V12/7/comer-j.html.

Delgado, J. (2004). Observations of public proceedings in Harris County Justice of the Peace Court, December 3, 2004.

Delgado, J. (2006). Interview conducted December 4, 2004 and February 1, 2006.

Downing, M. (2005, February 17). Mind reading. *Houston Press*. Retrieved July 3, 2005, from www.houstonpress.com.

Dubose, L. (1998, March 27). Deschooling society: Who's paying for public school vouchers? *The Texas Observer*, p. 4–7.

Fraga, D. (2004). Observations of public judicial proceedings in the City of Houston Municipal Teen Court, November 22, 2004.

Harris County. (2004). Workload study case filling statistics. Houston, TX: Harris County.

Harvard University Advancement Projects and Civil Rights Project. (2000). *Opportunities Suspended: The Devastating Consequences of Zero Tolerance and School Discipline*. Retrieved March 23, 2004, from www.civilrightsproject.harvard.edu/research/disci pline/opport_suspended.php.

Johnson, J. (2004). Why is school discipline considered a trivial issue? *Education Week*. Retrieved June 23, 2004, from www.edweek.org/ew/articles/2004/06/23/41johnson .h23.html.

Justice of the Peace Court Precinct 2, Harris County, Texas. (2005). *Students Overage by Grade Level: A Report to the Justice of the Peace Court Precinct 2.*

Pollock, M. (2004). *Colormute: Race Talk Dilemmas in an American School*. Princeton, NJ: Princeton University Press.

Rimer, S. (2004, January 4). Some unruly students now face arrest, not detention. *New York Times*, pp. A1, A15.

Rumbaut, R. G. (2005). Turning points in the transition to adulthood: Determinants of education attainment, incarceration, and early childbearing among children of immigrants. *Ethnic and Racial Studies* 28(6), 1041–1086.

State of Texas Judicial Report. (2004). *The Justice of the Peace Courts*. Austin, TX: Author, pp. 52–54.

Texas Education Agency. (2004). Accountability manual, 2004. Retrieved November 24, 2004, from www.tea.state.tx.us/perfreport/account/2004/manual/body.html.

Texas Education Code. §25.094(e). (2004).

Texas Education Code. §25.095(d). (2004) p. 154.

Texas Education Code. §37.104. (2004).

Texas Education Code. §37.107. (2004).

Texas Education Code. §39.0231. (2004).

Texas Education Code Annotated. §37.107. Vernon Supp. (2002).

Texas Education Code Annotated. §37.124. Vernon Supp. (2002).

Texas Education Code Annotated. §37.126. Vernon Supp. (2002).

Tyack, D. B. (1974). *The One Best System: A History of American Urban Education*. Cambridge, MA: Harvard University Press.

Vernon's Ann. Texas C.C.P. Art. 45.057. (2005).

Wald, J., and Losen, D. J. (2003). Defining and redirecting a school-to-prison pipeline. *New Directions for Youth Development* (fall 2003). San Francisco: Jossey-Bass.

5

A Battle Each Day: Teachers Talk about Discipline, Suspensions, and Zero Tolerance Policy

Johanna Wald and Ronnie Casella

We had 1,700 kids leave the community last year and 1,600 come in. We had 35 percent of the high school turnover straight transients. We had a first grade that had thirty in September, thirty in June, but not the same thirty. . . . We have seventy nations represented and over fifty languages spoken. We should be basically on fire but [we're not] because of the services and the staff and the police, the administration, the security of the teachers. I'll tell you, it's a battle each day.

In one short excerpt, this teacher from an urban high school in Connecticut offers some revealing glimpses into the daily struggles that teachers face. He talks about students who live in families that move frequently, speak different languages, and come from many parts of the world. He refers to classes where there is an almost 100 percent turnover rate during the course of the year. This teacher also equates his job with fighting a war (it's a battle each day) and with being "on fire."

Similar sentiments of feeling under siege and embattled were common responses that we received from many of the teachers that we met with in a series of focus groups about school discipline. Some equated their job with that of a prison warden and others with an emergency room doctor. We believe that their insights, perceptions, and attitudes help to shed light on the critical role that teachers play in maintaining discipline and in shaping the overall climate of a school. We also believe that their perspective on school discipline can be very useful and informative to school administrators who seek to create safe, orderly, and respectful school environments in which both students and teachers can thrive.

CONTEXT

During the past decade, a fierce debate has sprung up across the country over the use of "zero tolerance" policies in schools (Ayers, Dohrn, and Ayers,

2001). These policies mandate automatic suspensions and expulsions for a variety of offenses committed by students. As the range and variety of offenses covered under zero tolerance policies expanded in districts throughout the country, the number of students excluded from schools for at least one day each year skyrocket. Proponents of zero tolerance argue that these exclusions are necessary to maintain safety and order and to "keep learning in and trouble out" (Civil Rights Project, 2000). In Connecticut, for example, suspensions jumped about 90 percent between 1998–1999 and 2000–2001— from 57,626 to 90,559 (Gordon, 2003). Proponents of zero tolerance argue that these exclusions are necessary to maintain safe and orderly schools and to "keep learning in and trouble out." Opponents claim that they represent overly harsh responses to relatively minor misbehaviors, deny students an education, and disproportionately harm minority and poor students (Wald and Losen, 2003; Casella, 2003).

Teachers clearly play a pivotal role in the "disciplinary chain" that occurs in public schools. They frequently make the decision—often in a split second—whether to keep an incident contained within the classroom or whether to instigate the disciplinary referral that could lead to suspension or other sanctions. These decisions can be influenced by a variety of factors that have little to do with the actual behavior committed by the offending student. For example, in one study, researchers observed and videotaped classroom interactions, and found that a series of exchanges between different students and the teacher often preceded a "disciplinary moment" in which one student is singled out for punishment (Vavrus and Cole, 2002). The unlucky student had not necessarily committed the most egregious misbehavior but had, rather, challenged the teacher at the moment when he or she felt compelled to reassert his or her authority.

Yet, until recently, the voices of teachers have been surprisingly absent from the debate over zero tolerance. The two largest teachers unions—the National Educators Association (NEA) and the American Federation of Teachers (AFT)—have been split on this issue. They originally supported these policies but then withdrew their support. In the public arenas, this debate is often dominated by lawyers and student advocates on one hand and school and law enforcement officials on the other.

We initiated these focus groups in order to learn more about teachers' perspectives, experiences, and attitudes about how discipline is handled in their school.[1] We hoped to explore more fully how teachers felt about the use of suspensions as disciplinary tools and whether their attitudes toward school exclusions were related to the schools they taught in, the population of students they served, and the level of perceived support they received from administrators.

In the summer of 2004, shortly after we completed our focus groups, a report was released by Public Agenda (2004) entitled "Teaching Interrupted." Authors surveyed 725 middle and high school teachers about their views on school discipline. The report found widespread dissatisfaction among teachers about the amount of time they had to spend dealing with a few disruptive students. The report also noted that one third of teachers have considered leaving the profession because of discipline problems and that they think their schools should be doing a better job of responding to minor violations. Not surprisingly, according to this study, the vast majority of teachers (70 percent) surveyed support zero tolerance.

Our findings both differ from and expand upon the conclusions drawn from "Teaching Interrupted" in several significant ways. While our focus groups certainly uncovered a strong strand of support among teachers for school suspensions, we also encountered many teachers who objected to school exclusions in any but the most extreme circumstances. These teachers tended to recognize that suspending students "did not get at the root" of the problem and merely had the effect of further isolating that particular student. One teacher from an urban school called suspensions "death" to students who had no other safe havens in their lives.

In between these two extremes were the views of many teachers that suspensions would be less necessary if they had more counselors and service providers available to them and if they had more time and resources to devote to needy students. In other words, our focus groups, overall, provide evidence of a more nuanced attitude toward suspensions on the part of many teachers than these surveys might suggest. Because we were able to probe beyond initial support for zero tolerance, we discovered that, even among supporters of zero tolerance, many teachers recognized that suspensions represented an inadequate, largely negative, disciplinary measure that did not address the real causes of a student's misbehavior. Many expressed a desire for better and more counseling services to help troubled students, for more varied and graduated disciplinary options, and for more training in classroom management techniques to help them diffuse potentially volatile situations.

METHODOLOGY

We conducted five focus groups over the period of eight months for public school middle and high school teachers in Connecticut. We designed a set of questions that we piloted with a group of Massachusetts teachers. We decided to limit our teachers to middle and high school because this is where the overwhelming majority of suspensions and expulsions occur, and because disciplinary problems at this age group also differ markedly from those experienced at the elementary level.[2]

We tried to recruit a diverse range of teachers in terms of sex, race, and level of experience, and in terms of the schools in which they worked.[3]

KEY FINDINGS

We fully recognize that focus groups represent a first step of research, and that they cannot be considered representative or definitive. Nonetheless, we believe that the groups helped us to uncover some provocative points that should be known to administrators, educators, and politicians as they continue to amend and implement zero tolerance and other disciplinary policies and codes.

Deep Frustration with Inconsistent Administrators

In all but one focus group, teachers described dealing with inconsistent administrators as one of their biggest challenges. Many felt that a lack of communication and support from administration usurped their authority and sometimes led to unfair treatment of students. As one teacher explained, "There's this big inconsistency [with administrators] which I think is very bad and the kids pick up on that and they know."

Many felt as if they were not respected by administrators or had any real power or authority regarding discipline. In fact, several voiced uncertainty about whether there even was a zero tolerance policy in their school, because the attitudes and policies around discipline seemed to change on a regular basis. They often felt as if the administrators did not communicate these policy shifts very effectively. As a result, many chose to create their own disciplinary policies, opting to keep administrators out of the mix as much as possible.

> [I wish] I wouldn't have to feel afraid that if I sent this student to the office they would get suspended, but this student might not for doing the exact same thing in my classroom. You know, if so and so is swearing too much in class and I sent him out, he just might get suspended for five days, and that just might be the thing that makes him not want to come back to school. But [another] so and so can swear as much as he wants, and he's just going to go to the office and have a little talking to and come back to class. And so it's definitely an issue because it is something I have to think about before I say, "Go to the office." And that takes up my time and . . . my patience and ability to deal with the issue on my own level.

Table 5.1   Focus group schools and participants (2002/2003)*

Focus Groups	Details of Groups	School Demographics	Racial Composition of School
Group #1	9 teachers from schools in Connecticut: 2 men, 7 women, 8 white	Urban, suburban, and rural	
Group #2	7 teachers: 4 men, 3 women, all white	Urban/Suburban 2,333 students 87.2% grad. rate 63% attend post-secondary education 31.4% free/reduced lunch	38% White 31% Black 24% Hispanic 5% Asian
Group #3	7 teachers: 4 women, 3 men, 4 black, 3 white. Two of these teachers were from school #4.	Urban 1,271 students 1.3% free/reduced lunch	86.9% Black 10.4% Hispanic 1.8% White 0.03% Asian
Group #4	11 teachers: 7 women, 4 men, 3 black, 2 Asian, 6 white, from a charter that accepts students from across the district	Urban Charter 687 students 40% eligible for free/reduced lunch	56.5% Black 23.1% Hispanic 15.4% White 2% Asian
Group #5	9 teachers: 4 men, 5 women, all white	Suburban 1,365 Students 87.4% attend post–secondary education 16.1% eligible for free/reduced lunch	65.6% White 10.8% Black 9.3% Asian
Total	43 teachers: 17 men, 26 women, 7 black, 2 Asian, 1 Hispanic, 33 white		

*These figures came from reports from the schools required under No Child Left Behind.

Each of the schools that the teachers worked in had several administrators. Some of the schools were separated into "houses" and had principals (or masters) for each house. In these cases, teachers frequently noted that consistency between the different administrators was lacking. Echoing the sentiments of others, one teacher explained:

I'll tell you what the consequences would be [for a misbehaving student]: Administrator A is going to pat you on the back and say, "Don't do that again." Administrator B is going to probably call your parents, and C is just going to send you home for ten days, so I am very careful about who I send them to. We have three different assistant principals and the principal. They all have different philosophies. They are not consistent across the board. I mean, we have one really consistent, follows everything to a "t." We have another one that's making deals with the kids, undermines your authority.

The frustration expressed by these teachers is particularly interesting when one considers the findings of Russ Skiba and Heather Edl (2004), who surveyed principals in that state about their attitudes toward school discipline. The authors found these officials to be evenly divided over whether zero tolerance "sends a clear message to disruptive students about appropriate behavior in school." They identified principals who believed in prevention and used suspension only as a last resort, those who saw suspensions as their only disciplinary option and used it frequently, and those who used suspensions but also encouraged teachers to handle disciplinary problems in class whenever possible. Skiba and Edl concluded that the attitudes of the principals had more to do with whether a student is suspended than the actual behavior of the student.

Clearly, the teachers that we spoke with encountered all three types of administrators, often in the same school. This seemed to leave many confused and frustrated, and prompted several to simply take disciplinary matters into their own hands as much as possible.

Minor Violations and Zero Tolerance Policy

By and large, teachers did not express much fear about outright violence. Rather, they often expressed feeling worn down by the petty spats, swearing, and disrespect they observed in school every day. The major disciplinary issues identified by teachers were dress code violations, disrespect, insubordination, verbal abuse, offensive language, and minor altercations between students. As one teacher explained, "The problems in our school mainly come from he said/she said or problems in the community which exacerbate at the high school." Another noted that the problem is "students who are not interested in the course . . . it's language . . . loitering in the hallways . . . language in the hallways."

Dress code violations figured surprisingly prominently in many teachers' estimations. These were a major issue for many teachers and were consistently listed among the top two or three disciplinary problems that teachers faced on a regular basis. For youths, dress code violations appeared to be a gateway to larger disciplinary problems, since repeated violations led to increased sanctions, including suspensions. Dress code violations also led to showdowns between students and teachers.

> Our biggest concern is the students don't like [the dress code]. The boys have to have their shirts tucked. [Sometimes] the boys actually have it tucked in and the girls don't. So the boys will try to untuck it as much as they can and so we are constantly on them, "Please tuck in your shirt, please tuck in your shirt, please tuck in your shirt." First time warning. Second time a letter's sent home. Third time suspension. So that's one of our biggest concerns because we have kids who are getting suspended all the time because of it.

As one teacher explained, "We're not allowing students to wear blue jeans in the schools. If someone comes in wearing blue jeans, they just stick out from the class and we put them in school suspension. We call it 'in house.' And the next day, he is suspended from the school for one day." Another noted the same kind of issue, "If they are wearing hats or headbands, we take them off and they get 'in house' the next day. If they repeat it, they get suspended."

Yet, teachers pointed out that students sometimes had legitimate reasons for violating dress codes. One teacher explained that boys didn't like tucking in their shirts because doing so made them look fat. Another explained how a student did not want to take off his coat because he was embarrassed about the holes in his shirt.

Some teachers did not agree with all the attention that was given to these minor offenses, and disagreed with zero tolerance approaches that could end with a suspension in matters that seemed to them rather insignificant. As one teacher explained, "We have a no-hat rule, and the kids don't agree with why the rule is there and don't have any idea why they can't wear a hat so, to them, it's a stupid rule; so, they have a hard time following it."

Lack of Alternatives to Suspension

In several of the schools we visited, the sanctions of detention and in-school suspensions had been eliminated, leaving many teachers to believe that their choices were either "suspensions or nothing." The reasoning behind these decisions was problematic to some of the teachers.

> We don't have detention in this school. We have talked about it for a number of years, and one of the explanations [for not having it] was that they [the students] wouldn't come. What is it that they won't come to? I mean, so what if they have an afternoon job? If they have done wrong and they don't come, then give them the next penalty. But to just throw out the idea of a detention and not have one because they won't come, I think, is kind of silly.

Also, many teachers viewed in-school suspensions as "a joke" because it was a place where students could meet their friends and socialize. In some cases, school districts hire in-school and detention monitors who are paid minimum wage and are reluctant to enforce rules or make their own jobs difficult by keeping students quiet and focused. One teacher explained how their in-school suspension program operated.

> We had in-school suspension and what that turned into was socializing, sometimes playing cards, watching TV. They did anything and it became a place to go. . . . It got to the point where they wanted to go because it was a fun place, and to be suspended for some kids was a fun time because they don't have to be in school.

Another teacher highlighted one of the consequences of eliminating with in-school suspension. It feeds "external" suspensions and expulsions.

> We have done away with in-school suspensions, for the time being at least, just because they weren't being done the way that they were suppose to be done, and they weren't being done consistently, and they weren't a good punishment at that point. So we have done away with that for right now. We have a lot of externals.

"Soft" Support for Student Suspensions

While many teachers recognized the ineffectiveness of in-school suspension, they also voiced concerns about the impact on students of "externals"— outplacements, referrals to law enforcement, expulsions, and long-term suspensions. Many felt that they worsened problems for troubled students. "Suspensions alone, I don't think, are that effective. If it's undermined by the parents, if they really feel wronged, then the student comes back with an attitude, then it's repeated."

Nearly all of the teachers who supported the use of suspension and expulsion admitted that these sanctions were ineffective in addressing the problem behavior. Rather, many admitted to supporting zero tolerance policies because they made their own jobs easier and their classes more manageable. In short, they wanted a place to send students who were misbehaving or causing disruptions so they could get on with their work. At the same time, they knew that their way was the easy way out. As one teacher explained, "I think for them [it doesn't work], but for us it makes life sometimes easier when they are removed, because generally people who are getting suspended are repeaters."

What happened to "repeaters" once summoned by a guard or sent to the security office or principal was often not beneficial to the student, and teachers knew this. Almost all of the teachers felt that this was especially true for students who were constantly in trouble, those with the most problems and therefore in need of the greatest attention.

> Most of those kids who get constantly suspended . . . you see them on the attendance sheet. Every other week they're out for five days. But here, if you get suspended so many times, they just ship you out. [I had] about five kids in my class last year; when that happened, they [got] expelled. They'd get suspended, be out for five days, come back for two days, get expelled, suspended for five more days, and then, after the third or fourth time, they're gone. I mean, the kids who are like normally typically really good, that get suspended maybe once or twice and the parents really kill them, I mean it works for them. But the kids that have no support from home, they are repeat offenders. It doesn't matter. It just makes our lives easier in school because you are not dealing with them, but for them, no, [suspension doesn't help].

Many teachers recognized that some of their students needed counseling services far beyond their capacity. They also understood the relationship between lack of resources and the acting out behavior of some students. At the same time, they felt resigned to the fact that their schools were simply not equipped to handle students with so many problems.

> There are not enough social workers. There are not enough resources and I wonder how many students have fallen through the cracks, where they have behavioral problems because maybe they have some sort of learning disability, but they were not diagnosed so they can't really understand or read the book properly; so, therefore, instead of trying to get help, they are acting out.

Two teachers from other schools explain as follows:

> There are big, complex problems that are outside the school that are acted out in the school. And, I think one reason schools can't do it successfully [is] because sometimes when we find out what the real issues are, it's almost too late. The kid is on the second or third suspension. We didn't find out all of those factors involved, just listed, soon enough to address them.

> There's a lot of anger—even around people who are there to help; there's no recognition of it. There's so much pain there and that's what we're dealing with. And suspensions really only address the outside, not the root of the problem . . . . Usually, by the time you know it, so much damage has been done already. But, that's what maybe a large part of the public realize . . . the pain in certain families that they're dealing with . . . very, very, very, very difficult.

Most welcomed the idea of putting more counselors, services, and programs into their school, and valued the programs that did exist. One teacher referred to the advantages of a "full-service" school. "A full service school

. . . becomes more of a working environment where you're caring for the whole student, rather than just the academic needs of the student. I think that that's something that's very hard to do, but something that works very well." Another teacher discussed a school-based clinic that seemed helpful in helping students.

> We also have another option here because we have a school-based clinic. We can refer students that we think perhaps might need anger management; I think that's very good, and some of the students have already signed themselves up. They know. And I think that's a big plus to diffuse discipline problems. If they're angry, they're angry, and it's going to spill over into the classroom.

Other teachers had similar thoughts about their schools' violence prevention and conflict resolution programs, even when expressed in rather harsh tones. "I had kids who were ninth graders who I didn't think were going to make it past the first two months and I thought they were assassins. They're going to college now. That's because of teachers like this and programs that we have in place here."

Language Differences among Teachers

In one focus group, teachers described students as having "no respect for teachers, peers," as being "a repeat—again, same kid, always with her mouth in trouble all the time" and of special education students who "hide behind that label" so that they can misbehave. They spoke of "lockdowns" and "in houses" and "repeaters." In response to an incident of fighting, one teacher spoke of his hopes that a couple of students "with nice thick discipline files" will be given the maximum penalty of 180-day expulsion.

In marked contrast, a much more "caring" ethos was evident in a focus group in another school. Here students were described as "fragile." The focus from many of these teachers was on reaching out and saving these students, as evident from the following exchange:

> TEACHER A: It is like an emergency room in a hospital. We do triage. Kids come in and they are ailing, and we try to get them back in the population. It's an ambulatory walk-in center.
> TEACHER B: We don't cut the kids head off the first time, and I think that's important. I think that once the kids get a chance, they feel like they are being persecuted enough by their parents, by every other agency they are involved with. . . . It may take them awhile; it's like a stray dog, he is going to growl and bark at you, but if you get to know the dog, then you've got a friend for life, and I think that is what happens here.

TEACHER C: The kids know you care about them; [if] you talk to them like people, they will [know], I mean, over the years. I don't know how many kids we have been able to save—bottom line—save their lives because other kids felt they could talk to a certain teacher or something.

Coincidentally, half of the teachers in the first group taught at the middle school that fed students into the high school where the second group took place. So, these differences cannot be explained either by the disciplinary policies impacting those schools or by the population of students served. Thus, a very interesting question to ask is what might account for these very different perspectives, and even views of the role of teachers?

Two clues that may be worthy of further investigation can be gleaned from the responses of teachers in these groups. One involves the administration's attitudes toward school discipline. In the first group, the teachers voiced dissatisfaction over the administration's lack of consistency and what they perceived as a lack of support. In the second group, the teachers participating in the focus group were clearly more philosophically aligned with their administrators in their attitudes and approaches to school discipline. This school had developed a culture—supported at the top—which stressed using suspensions only as a last resort. Teachers in this school seemed to be trained and versed in this ethos and may, in fact, self-select to teach there because the administration's ideology is consistent with their own.

A second factor may be that teachers in the second group could send disruptive or troubled students out of the classroom without suspending them. There was a counseling center staffed by social workers and graduate students from nearby universities where students could work out conflicts with other students. Thus, they could obtain relief from potentially volatile classroom situations without sacrificing their students' needs. Equally important, these teachers indicated that all parties—students, teachers, and administrators—bought into the value of such a program (disclaimer: this has not been independently evaluated; this was simply the opinion expressed by the teachers participating in the focus group). "Instead of fighting in the hallway or fighting in the cafeteria, they know where they can come, and it is an accepted form and it's not a way to punk out. . . . It's 'Okay, let's go up to the center and let's work it out,' and it is a win win not a win lose."

We've had . . . a 50 percent reduction the first year, since we have had these programs. . . . It was a way to lose before, and it got into a lot of verbal and physical confrontations because they didn't have a place to address these issues. Now we have a place where they can sit and talk about it. . . . Before, ten years ago, before we had the center, you could almost feel the pressure in the hallways.

In another school, a teacher voiced support for a similar program.

> We also have another option here because we have a school-based clinic; we can
> refer students that we think perhaps might need anger management, and I think
> that's very good and some of the students have already signed themselves up. They
> know. And I think that's a big plus to diffuse discipline problems. If they're angry,
> they're angry, and its going to spill over into the classroom.

Thus, one theory worthy of further attention is that, when teachers are able
to remove disrupting students without punishing or suspending them, they are
inclined to do so, and to be less supportive of punitive policies that exclude
such students from school altogether. When teachers feel supported by their
administration and by such resources, they may be able to more easily consider the needs of both their students and themselves.

ADDITIONAL IDEAS FOR ADMINISTRATORS

Communicate with Teachers about Disciplinary Policies

Over and over again, we heard from teachers who felt disrespected, who felt
as if policies were being imposed on them without clear guidelines and without consistency, and who felt as if administrators were not backing them up.
Teachers seemed to bristle particularly at being questioned by administrators
in front of students. Just as many teachers spoke of the importance of making
sure that students do not "lose face," it is important for administrators to
make sure that teachers do not feel attacked, disrespected, or undermined,
particularly in front of students.

We were also surprised to learn that many teachers did not even know if
their school had a zero tolerance policy or, if it did, what it said. Several
mentioned that the disciplinary codes were changing with such regularity that
they had no idea what the official policy regarding discipline was. The lack
of consistency, or even knowledge, about official policies appears to be a
source of great stress for teachers. They resent feeling in the dark about these
issues, as well as having no voice in the formation of policies.

Devise More Creative and Varied Disciplinary Options

In some instances, we noted that teachers did not support suspensions as
much as they did the idea that students face some consequences for their
actions. Many felt that existing sanctions, such as in-school suspensions,
were meaningless or even counterproductive. As previously noted, many
schools have abolished both in-school suspension and detention, thus limiting

options for any sanctioning beside external suspensions. Even teachers who supported zero tolerance recognized that the sanctions associated with it—suspension, expulsion, arrest—were not particularly effective; however, they were seeking some relief to make their own jobs more manageable.

Many of the teachers we spoke with expressed the desire for more or better programs, counselors, and support to help troubled students. Their resignation and frustration with some students (and ultimate support for zero tolerance policy) often stemmed from the fact that they felt that schools were simply not currently equipped to handle students with multiple problems. In many ways, teachers felt overwhelmed, as if they did not have the time, know-how, or patience to deal with the kinds of problems many students possessed. Nonetheless, many expressed concern for these students and a desire for them to receive better services.

Based on what teachers said in this regard, it was obvious that more creative forms of discipline—that is, peer mediation, restorative justice, anger management, and conflict resolution—are desperately needed in high schools. Devising these could represent a wonderful way to involve both teachers and students in a school's policymaking and foster a more cooperative environment. There will always be conflicts when thousands of young people and hundreds of adults are in a building for seven hours each day. If there were no programs, initiatives, and people to deal with these conflicts, they would often escalate and give the impression that there is nothing to do but implement zero tolerance.

Rethink or Abolish Dress Code Statutes

We were, frankly, surprised and dismayed by the prominence of dress code violations among the list of major disciplinary issues faced by teachers. These consistently appeared among the top two or three disciplinary problems faced by the teachers that we spoke to and often were the cause of significant struggles between teachers and students. Yet, as previously discussed, students' objections to dress codes often seemed quite reasonable: they did not want to look fat in front of their friends, they didn't understand why they couldn't wear hats, or they were embarrassed by the holes in the shirts under their coats.

Moreover, we find it extremely counterproductive to suspend students—and thereby deny them an education and accelerate their alienation from, and failure in, school—because of their dress. Suspensions are a leading predictor of dropping out, and dropout rates are rising in most states. Many schools need to do a better job of reaching out to troubled students whose only chance for success in life is linked to their ability to complete high school. Pushing students out the door because of rigid dress code statutes does not, in our opinion, serve the interests of the students, the school, or society at large. Moreover, teachers voice considerable stress about enforcing these codes and having to play "dress police." These codes seem to put one more obstacle in the path of teachers who seek to create more positive relationships with their students.

Implement Counseling and Other Services That Can Relieve Teachers without Excluding Students

We noted a "soft" support for zero tolerance among many teachers, in that they recognized this response did not really help students or get to the root of student misbehaviors. At the same time, they expressed the need at times for relief from chronically disruptive students. They also supported violence-prevention programs, primarily because they felt that such programs did get to the root of the problem. In many ways, for teachers, zero tolerance was a short-term solution, solving the problem of disruptive students in school by getting them out of the way. Violence prevention—such as peer mediation, conflict-resolution training, and mentoring programs—was a long-term solution that depended on strong programs and caring teachers and administrators.

Interestingly, in the school where there was a structured vehicle for dealing with these conflicts—a formal, established program where students were sent to work out conflicts with counselors and social workers—the support among teachers for zero tolerance was low. This is also the school where teachers spoke most compassionately about their students, referring to them as "fragile" and stressing the importance of helping them to "save face" in their interactions with teachers and students.

Offer Classroom Management Training for Teachers

If there was one area of uniform agreement among all the teachers that we spoke to, it was the need for additional training in classroom management. Even those strongly supporting zero tolerance indicated that they would welcome additional support and training around how to diffuse potentially volatile situations and how to create more harmonious classroom interactions. Yet, many indicated that they had few opportunities for such training and that they felt more pressure to raise test scores than to improve the school and classroom climate (see also Stein, 2001).

CONCLUSIONS

Obviously, focus groups can only begin to shed light or illuminate some of the key issues that need to be further pursued. But it is clear from the focus groups we held that teachers do not support zero tolerance or suspensions because they think they are effective. While many believed that one suspension may actually scare a "good kid" and thus act as a deterrent, almost all agreed that suspensions were meaningless for "repeaters." However, many seemed resigned to "that's the way it is." There was a general sense that, as teachers, they could reach out to a certain extent but that some students had needs that were beyond their ability to help.

Many of the teachers we spoke with felt under siege. They not only have to teach in the classroom, but must also manage hallway transitions and enforce dress codes. Many do not feel as if their administrators back them up or even bother to communicate very well with them. The views expressed by many teachers in our focus groups suggest that, if teachers felt more respected by the administrators, and if they had more support and help dealing with difficult students, they might be less inclined to support exclusionary punishments for students.

NOTES

1. Funding for this project came from the Soros Foundation. Nan Stein, senior scientist at the Wellesley Center for Research on Women, served as the principal investigator for this research project. Dr. Stein helped to design the questions, ran the focus groups, analyzed data, and presented findings at several conferences.

2. There were at least two researchers at each focus group. We split the questions in half, with one of us leading the discussion for the first half and the other for the second half. We both took notes throughout the sessions. We tried to interrupt only if we needed clarification. We did not inject ourselves into the discussion or make known our own views about these issues. Our goal was to create a safe atmosphere where teachers felt free to express their opinions confidentially. We told all groups that, while final reports would discuss general themes and comments, no individual schools or teachers would be identified. After conducting three groups, we decided to shorten the questionnaire because we found ourselves rushing through the final questions in order to finish within a reasonable period of time. We decided to allow the teachers more time to respond to the questions. Often, during the second half of each focus group the

3. The first group consisted of nine teachers who were also master-level graduate students at a state university in Connecticut. They came from a range of districts throughout the state. Several were from the same middle school that serendipitously happened to be the feeder middle school for the high school teachers represented in our second focus group. Two taught at high security institutions designed for students already in the juvenile justice system. We have not included their responses because we did not feel that they

represented the population we were trying to reach, which was primarily teachers in mainstream public middle and high schools. The other four groups were comprised of teachers at the school where we held the focus groups, with the exception of one group where two of the seven teachers came from a nearby high school (see table 5.1).

REFERENCES

Ayers, W., Dohrn, B., and Ayers, R., eds. (2001). *Zero Tolerance: Resisting the Drive for Punishment in Our Schools.* New York: The New Press.

Casella, R. (2003). Punishing dangerousness through preventative detention: Illustrating the institutional link between school and prison. *New Directions for Youth Development 99,* 55–70.

The Civil Rights Project and the Advancement Project. (2000). *Opportunities Suspended: The Devastating Consequences of School Discipline and Zero Tolerance Policies.* Available at www.civilrightsproject.harvard.edu/research/discipline/discipline_gen.php.

Gordon, J. (2003, November 16). Connecticut: In schools, bad behavior is shown the door. *New York Times,* p. 1A.

Public Agenda. (2004, May). Teaching interrupted: Do discipline policies in today's public schools foster the common good? Prepared by Public Agenda with support from Common Good, www.publicagenda.org.

Skiba, R., and Edl, H. (2004). *The Disciplinary Practices Survey: How Do Indiana's Principals Feel about Discipline?* Bloomington: Indiana University, Center for Evaluation and Education Policy.

Stein, N. (2001). Sexual harassment meets zero tolerance: Life in K–12 schools. In W. Ayers, B. Dohrn, and R. Ayers (eds.), *Zero Tolerance: Resisting the Drive for Punishment in Our Schools* (pp. 143–154). New York: The New Press.

Vavrus, R., and Cole, K. M. (2002). "I didn't do nothin'": The discursive construction of school suspension. *The Urban Review 34,* 87–111.

Wald, J., and Losen, D. (2003). Defining and redirecting a school-to-prison pipeline. *New Directions for Youth Development 99,* 9–16.

6

Exclusion Is Not the Only Alternative: The Children Left Behind Project

M. Karega Rausch and Russell J. Skiba

Current evidence strongly suggests that the philosophy and practice of zero tolerance school discipline has failed as an educational intervention to ensure student safety, improve school climates, advance student learning, or provide equitable results; yet, the approach remains popular among many educational administrators and political leaders. The popularity of zero tolerance, however, does not mean that all educational leaders ascribe to this paradigm. Absent from much of the research base to date are the voices of school principals actively promoting alternative philosophies and practices better suited to meet the paramount goals of student safety and learning. This chapter describes the findings of the Children Left Behind project, focusing on the perspectives and practices of school leaders in one midwestern state. The emerging results of this project suggest that (1) diversity exists among school principals in their endorsement of zero tolerance school discipline, (2) the disciplinary perspectives of school principals are related to the use of exclusionary student removal and use of preventive alternatives, and (3) the perspective of principals endorsing alternatives to student exclusion suggest that removing students from the learning environment is not the only method available for keeping students safe to learn.

Out-of-school suspension and expulsion are widely used in our schools, and their frequency is increasing. Our best evidence to date shows that suspension and expulsion are among the most widely used disciplinary techniques, perhaps the most frequently used disciplinary tools (Bowditch, 1993;

Mansfield and Farris, 1992; Rose, 1988; Skiba, Peterson, and Williams, 1997; Uchitelle, Bartz, and Hillman, 1989). National data estimate that about 7 percent of the school population missed at least one day of school due to being suspended or expelled, double the number since the 1970s (U.S. Department of Education, 2000; Wald and Losen, 2003). Further, large and widening racial disparities are evident in the composition of students removed from school; in 2000, while representing 17 percent of the student population, African Americans represented 34 percent of the suspended population (U.S. Department of Education, 2000; Wald and Losen, 2003). African American students are currently 2.6 times as likely to be suspended compared to white students, up from about two times as likely in the 1970s (U.S. Department of Education, 2000; Wald and Losen, 2003).

Scholars have suggested that the surge and growing inequity in student removal is due in part to the emergence and popularity of the philosophy termed "zero tolerance" (Ayers, Dohrn, and Ayers, 2001; Noguera, 1995; Skiba and Peterson, 1999; Verdugo, 2002; Wald and Losen, 2003). In short, zero tolerance school discipline is based on the assumption of *deterrence*: irrespective of context, punishing school "troublemakers" severely sends a message that misbehavior will not be tolerated, and schools will be more orderly and safer for those remaining. The philosophy assumes that distributing uniform punishments and removing disruptive students will yield safer schools, improved climates more conducive to learning, and more equitable distribution of punishment (Skiba, 2004).

Although intuitively appealing, our best evidence has failed to support the assumptions of zero tolerance. Zero tolerance in general and suspension and expulsion in particular have been associated with a number of negative schooling outcomes including higher rates of dropout (Bowditch, 1993), a more punitive schooling environment (Bickel and Qualls, 1980), high rates of repeat offending (Tobin, Sugai, and Colvin, 1996), and increased racial inequality without any evidence of higher rates of misbehavior in minority student populations (Skiba et al., 2002; Wald and Losen, 2003). Frequent use of student exclusion has also been found to be related to lower achievement on state accountability examinations, even after controlling for other strong sociodemographic predictors of achievement (Davis and Jordan, 1994; Raffaele Mendez, Knoff, and Ferron, 2002; Rausch, Skiba, and Simmons, 2005). Further, emerging evidence suggests that zero tolerance strengthens a school-to-prison pipeline by criminalizing student misbehavior that would normally have been addressed by school officials (Advancement Project, 2005; Wald and Losen, 2003).

In spite of the evidence suggesting the ineffectiveness of zero tolerance school discipline, it remains a popular approach advocated by many political leaders and educational administrators. Recent evidence at the national, state, and school-district levels have demonstrated large surges in the number and percent of students being suspended and expelled from school, often coinciding with the implementation of zero tolerance policies (Advancement Project, 2005; Gordon, Della Piana, and Keleher, 2001; Harvard Civil Rights Project, 2000; Michigan Public Policy Institute, 2003; Potts et al., 2003; Richart, Brooks, and Soler, 2003). The popularity is also illustrated by state legislatures and local school districts broadening the mandate of zero tolerance beyond the federal mandates of firearms (i.e., the Gun-Free Schools Act of 1994; Public Law 103-227, 1994) to drugs and alcohol, fighting, and threats or swearing. Many school boards continue to toughen their disciplinary policies; some have begun to experiment with permanent expulsion from the system for some offenses. Others have begun to apply school suspensions, expulsions, or transfers to behaviors that occur outside of school (Ayers et al., 2001; Michigan Public Policy Initiative, 2003; Potts et al., 2003).

Yet the current popularity of zero tolerance school discipline does not mean that all educational leaders ascribe to this paradigm, including those serving student populations assumed to be at a higher risk for school removal (Harvard Civil Rights Project, 2000; Dunbar and Villarruel, 2004; Mukuria, 2002; Raffaele Mendez et al., 2002). Absent from much of the research literature to date are the perspectives and practices of school leaders explicitly advocating an approach that favors preventive alternatives to student removal. Consistent with a growing research base suggesting that prevention is more effective than removal (Dwyer, Osher, and Warger, 1998; Elliott et al., 2001; Gagnon and Leone, 2001; Mihalic et al., 2001; Thornton et al., 2000), these voices-in-practice offer much to the dialogue on how best to ensure safe and productive learning environments for students.

There is no debate that schools must be places that preserve, maintain, and create climates conducive to learning for *all* students, and disciplinary systems must facilitate progress toward these goals. The question that creates controversy is *how* to create disciplinary systems supportive of these ends. The large and growing research base suggests that student exclusion as a primary part of a school's disciplinary system has been unable to help educators meet these goals. Thus, alternative perspectives and practices from those engaged with students every day are of paramount importance. This chapter seeks to fill this gap, by describing some of the findings of the Children Left Behind project,[1] illustrating that many school leaders believe that preventive disciplinary systems are best suited to achieve the goal of creating school climates conducive to learning.

THE CHILDREN LEFT BEHIND PROJECT

The goals of the Children Left Behind project were twofold: (1) to open a statewide dialogue concerning the best methods for promoting and maintaining a safe and productive learning climate in the schools of this midwestern state, and (2) to initiate and maintain a forum for discussion between those in the juvenile justice system and the state's educational system to ensure that methods chosen for maintaining order in our schools do not jeopardize the human potential of young people or the overall safety of communities. The project was guided by two foundational principles: (1) schools have a right and responsibility to apply methods that are effective in maintaining a climate that is as free as possible of disruptions to student learning, and (2) best practice suggests, and recent federal policy mandates (i.e., the No Child Left Behind Act; Public Law 107-110, 2002), that all educational practices employed in schools must maximize the opportunity to learn for all children, regardless of their background.

In the following sections, we describe the data from the Children Left Behind project, highlighting the perspectives-in-practice of local principals in creating and maintaining safe and productive schools. First, we describe results from a survey of school principals, querying their attitudes about the purpose, process, and outcomes of school discipline. Next, the results of in-depth interviews with principals describing preventive practices used in their schools are presented. One of these interviews, describing how a preventive approach can have a transformative effect on the schooling environment, is described in more detail.

PRINCIPAL PERSPECTIVES ON SCHOOL DISCIPLINE: THE DISCIPLINARY PRACTICES SURVEY

A common misconception held by some educators and policy makers is that there are virtually no alternatives to school removal for maintaining safe schools. However, surveys with principals in this midwestern state suggest that a diversity of perspectives, opinions, and activities exist within schools.

A survey of 325 school principals was conducted in the state of Indiana to better understand principal attitudes towards school discipline (Skiba and Edl, 2004). The survey was administered in an online format during March and April of 2003. Principals were asked to rate their agreement with statements reflecting various attitudes about school discipline. Principals were also asked to rate usage of a number of preventive disciplinary strategies (e.g., bullying prevention, conflict resolution, etc.) in their schools.

Results revealed that principals hold very different perspectives on school discipline. Principals were almost evenly split over whether zero tolerance "sends a clear message to disruptive students about appropriate behavior in schools." Further, a large majority (98.5 percent) of principals thought that "teachers ought to be able to manage the majority of students' misbehavior in their classrooms." Yet, only 29 percent thought that teachers were adequately trained by their teacher training programs to deal with student misbehavior.

Further statistical analysis revealed three distinct perspectives on school discipline among these principals (see table 6.1). These clusters were categorized as prevention orientation, support for suspension and expulsion, and pragmatic prevention. Importantly, differences in principal perspectives were not only associated with use of suspension but were also related to attitudes regarding parents, students, and special education disciplinary regulations.

Table 6.1   Representative items endorsed more frequently by principals with different perspectives on school discipline*

Group1: Prevention Orientation
- Developing and implementing prevention programs pays off in terms of decreased disruption and disciplinary incidents.
- Suspension and expulsion do not really solve disciplinary problems.
- Students with disabilities who engage in disruptive behavior need a different approach to discipline than students in general education.
- I feel it is critical to work with parents before suspending a student from school.
- Conversations with students referred to the office should be factored into most decisions about disciplinary consequences.

Group 2: Support for Suspension and Expulsion
- Zero tolerance makes a significant contribution to maintaining order at my school.
- Out-of-school suspension is a necessary tool for maintaining school order.
- Most if not all disciplinary problems come from inadequacies in the child's home situation.
- Disciplinary regulations for special education create a separate system that makes it more difficult to enforce discipline.
- My duties as an administrator simply don't allow me the time to get to know students on an individual basis.

Group 3: Pragmatic Prevention
- Suspension and expulsion allow students time away from school that encourages them to think about their behavior.
- Teachers at this school were adequately prepared to handle problems of misbehavior and discipline.
- *Least likely to believe that*: Regardless of whether it is effective, suspension is virtually our only option.
- *Least likely to believe that*: Violence is getting worse at my school.

*Unless otherwise noted, items listed are those that the group in question on average rated the highest of the three groups, and significantly higher than at least one other group.

For example, the one third of responding principals supporting a preventive approach to discipline were also more likely to believe that it is critical to work with parents before suspension, that discipline should be adapted to meet the needs of students with disabilities, and that conversations with students are an important part of the disciplinary process. This cluster of principals served schools with fewer suspensions for both serious infractions (e.g., drugs, weapons) and general disruptive behavior, and were more likely to report having conflict resolution, individual behavior plans, peer mediation, bullying prevention, and anger management programs in place.

In contrast, one third of the principals supported the use of suspension and expulsion and agreed that zero tolerance makes a significant contribution to maintaining order at their school. They were also more likely to believe that discipline problems stem from an inadequate home situation, that special education disciplinary regulations create a separate system that makes it more difficult to enforce discipline, and that they lack sufficient time to get to know students on an individual basis. These principals served schools with higher rates of out-of-school suspension.

The final group of principals that emerged might be termed a "pragmatic prevention" group. On the one hand, these principals agreed that out-of-school suspension and expulsion encourage students to think about their behavior, but they are also least likely to believe that suspension and expulsion were their only options and were least likely to believe that school violence was increasing at their school. The attitudes expressed by this group tended to fall somewhere in-between the first two groups. They also more closely resembled the prevention orientation group, with a lower rate of suspension and a higher reported use of prevention programs than principals who supported suspension and expulsion.

Thus, consistent with previous research (Harvard Civil Rights Project, 2000; Morrison, Morrison, and Minjarez, 1999; Raffaele Mendez et al., 2002), there appear to be important differences among principals in their beliefs about school discipline. In the following sections, we explore these perspectives in more detail, presenting interviews with principals who have chosen a more preventive approach to discipline for maintaining a safe and productive school climate.

ALTERNATIVE PERSPECTIVES AND ACTIONS TO
ZERO TOLERANCE SCHOOL DISCIPLINE

In order to come to a deeper understanding of the choices that principals make at the school level, the Children Left Behind project interviewed principals across the state who described a variety of options they use as an alternative to zero tolerance suspensions and expulsions.[2] Principals participating in the study were solicited through the state association of school principals and volunteered to share information about programs in their schools that they feel are effective in maintaining a safe and productive learning climate. Protocols were developed and used querying the following areas: (1) philosophy/program description (e.g., what is the school's disciplinary philosophy, who does the program serve, where is it located, etc.), (2) structure (e.g., what methods are used to prevent violence and disruption from occurring or intervene when they do occur), and (3) outcomes (e.g., how have students and staff responded to this philosophy/program).

Telephone interviews were conducted with nine principals and one high school assistant principal responsible for discipline. Interviews lasted approximately one and a half hours. All interviews were audio recorded and transcribed for accuracy. Transcribed interview data were analyzed for trends and themes (Silverman, 2000; Yin, 2003) specific to programs, practices, and perspectives that participants reported using to maintain safe and productive schools. Three researchers analyzed the data independently and then came to a consensus on the most relevant, recurring, and informative themes and trends.

Across conversations with principals serving a diversity of schools, three primary themes emerged: (1) the necessity of intervening proactively rather than reactively, (2) an emphasis on building and strengthening connections with students, especially those placed at risk, and (3) utilizing creative options to suspension and expulsion, even for the most extreme behavior. Each of these themes is described in turn below.

Proactive Intervention

Principals stressed the importance of promoting a common understanding among staff, students, parents, and administrators of how discipline works at their schools. These principals work closely with their teachers to define what the most appropriate referrals to the office are and which are better handled at the classroom level.

> "We went through some scenarios—for example, a child taking a pencil away from another child—that should never come to the office. A child who intentionally is trying to hurt another child—that directly comes to the office. . . . My philosophy has always been you settle it at the lowest level."

Principals suggested that this approach actually gives teachers more authority in their classrooms.

> Once you send a child to the office, as a classroom teacher you give up a part of
> your control over that child. . . . So, I think as a school we've come to realize that
> it's a lot better to handle the discipline within the team [of teachers] if we can
> because that sends a message to the student that the team has control.

Such an approach also frees up administrator time, noted the principals, from
having to deal with an endless stream of referrals to more time for counseling
students or meeting for planning with teacher teams.

These schools also reported involving parents throughout the disciplinary
process. At a number of schools, teachers contact parents before any referral
to the office is made. In one school, parents are actively encouraged to support the school's disciplinary code early in the year:

> "At the beginning of the year, I had the child sign [the code of conduct card], and I
> had the parents sign it. . . . At our back-to-school meeting, I shared with the parents
> that I was asking for their support."

As a result of such communication, parents tend to be more supportive of
school disciplinary actions, as this urban elementary school principal notes,

> "I have very few parents who get upset with me because a lot of times we've done
> a lot of interventions. . . . There are no surprises. And, I have to think the parents
> appreciate that because they've been part of it through the entire process."

Building Meaningful Relationships with Students, Especially Those Placed At Risk

School alienation has been found to be a risk factor for both juvenile delinquency (Elliot, Hamburg, and Williams, 1998) and deadly school violence
(Vossekuil et al., 2002). For those students whose behavior indicates a higher
risk for disruption, principals suggested that they worked hard to establish
communication with students. One high school administrator noted,

> We're very hands-on administrators. I think that the students feel like they can come
> to us at any time and work with us. We go to a lot of student activities, a lot more
> than I know most administrators do, just trying to be present and let the students
> know that we really do care, and we try to work with them. That's not a program;
> that's just kind of a philosophy that we have.

As a result, these administrators believe that students are more willing to
communicate potential problems to staff and administrators in the building.
An assistant principal in a suburban high school described the school's
attempts to keep channels of communication open:

> "Every time he [the principal] has the student body together, he reminds them that if there is anything out there that's lingering and dangerous to make sure that you bring it forward. He just continually impresses upon the kids how important communication is."

Trust of administrators proved critical in this building: when a student approached the administration to report a student with a cache of weapons, administrators and local police were able to take preventive action that headed off a potentially deadly situation (*Herald Times*, 2001).

Mentoring programs, such as the Big Brothers/Big Sisters program have been identified as among the most effective programs for reducing the risk of violence (Mihalic et al., 2001). At one urban elementary school, every adult, from administrators to teachers to custodial staff, was asked to mentor one child who had been identified as someone "who we considered to be disconnected from school."

> And all we asked was that the adults would meet with these kids once a week . . . I would have lunch with this child, and we would play chess and we would talk . . . We saw that we were making progress with these kids because really a lot of these kids didn't have anyone who really took an interest in them.

Many of the principals remarked on the relationship for many students between risk for academic failure and risk for acting-out behavior. One administrator in a suburban high school described the relationship between academic and behavioral problems this way:

> Some behavioral problems are due to [a student's] feeling inadequate in the classroom or feeling as if they can't perform academically—"I'd rather be bad than dumb." That [understanding] has really helped us a lot. . . . We have alleviated that problem by trying to keep kids from feeling that way in whatever setting they are in.

Creative Alternatives to Student Removal

By no means were the principals we talked with inclined to in any way relax their expectations for appropriate behavior. Suspension and expulsion were by no means ruled out as an option for seriously disruptive behavior.

> We will not put up with misbehavior. . . . You are here to learn, and we're going to do everything we can to provide the proper education. Your teachers are here to work with you. We're doing everything we can to support you, but then again we will not deal with any misbehaviors. That's the bottom line. If you hit somebody, you're going to be suspended.

Yet the principals we interviewed also typically rejected a one-size-fits-all disciplinary approach. As one elementary school principal noted,

> "We don't have a zero tolerance policy. . . . In the office, we really seek to understand what's going on and have consequences that make sense. [We] try not to use out-of-school suspensions unless we're at our wits' end. We want them here at school."

Trying to achieve this balance seems to lead these principals to an approach wherein the severity of punishment is more likely tailored to fit the seriousness of the infraction. According to one principal,

> "Just to have a standard, people say, 'Well, okay, you lose a recess no matter what the infraction is.' But let's say they have written on a wall in the bathroom. I think they should put on gloves and clean it off. That makes sense."

Perhaps most striking were the creative ways in which these schools modified the traditional notions of out-of-school suspension and expulsion to send a strong disciplinary message to students without reducing (and perhaps even increasing) their time in school. One high school uses what they term "probationary expulsion" for nondangerous offenses.

> We absolutely do not believe in zero tolerance policies. . . . If we're going to expel a student, probably 90 percent of the time we will expel him or her technically but we allow the student to return to school on what's called a continuing education agreement. . . . What we're trying to do is make a commitment to try to help kids, to allow them, even though they've made a pretty major mistake, for example possession of drugs or alcohol . . . to return to school on a probationary basis. It is very proactive because for the student's benefit we require drug testing and counseling as a part of that.

The principals we spoke with reported that a combination of high expectations and support for students can be effective even for the toughest kids. As one high school disciplinarian noted,

> We've had several really tough kids enter this school, and after going through and being surrounded by kids who have embraced the class and the culture of the school they've turned it around. We're not seeing that aggressive behavior. Because they know this is a nurturing place. They know that the teachers care about them as individuals. Other classmates care about them . . . that has helped eliminate many of the problems.

PREVENTION-IN-ACTION: THE GREENFIELD MIDDLE SCHOOL TRANSFORMATION

A story of transformation especially intriguing to the interviewing staff of the Children Left Behind project is that of Greenfield Middle School under the leadership of Jim Bever, the 2004 Metlife/National Association of Secondary School Principals and Indiana Middle School principal of the year honoree. Greenfield's story illustrates that implementation of preventive alternatives in schools can have profound positive outcomes for students. What follows is a brief summary of that interview,[3] and supporting documentation of the effectiveness of the innovative approaches implemented at Greenfield.

The Disciplinary Climate at Greenfield

Discipline prior to Bever's accepting the principalship seemed to be consistent with the zero tolerance philosophy of punishing even minor student misbehavior severely in an attempt to "send a message" to students.

> The atmosphere in the building was one of demanded respect as opposed to earned respect. Comments from students, sometimes inappropriate in nature, were often considered disrespectful and punished as a violation of the schools expectation of respect. There was little delineation between behavior that was inappropriate and in violation of the school's conduct code and behavior that teachers found distasteful or personally objectionable. Both types of behaviors were severely punished when referred to the office. There was a common understanding that students must suffer as a result of punishment.

Further, the disciplinary climate at this middle school was less than optimal, as evidenced by some serious acts of violence and a heavy reliance on school administrators to deal with student behavior.

> We were seeing 300 plus office referrals a month in 1998 and 1999. . . . There were some fairly violent acts occurring in this building. . . . The year prior to me coming to this building, there was even a student who had been so severely beaten she lost continence and was taken out on an ambulance cot. So things were not very good here when I came.

The high levels of office referrals, suspensions, and expulsions seemed to be due, not to any inherent desire to remove students from schools, so much as not knowing what else to do. This is evidenced by a conversation between a teacher and Bever.

"This is the only thing I've ever known. The first principal that I worked under told me you have to put a kid up against the wall now and then to get their attention. . . . It's the only thing I knew in my high school career and it's the only thing I know now." So I told him, "Okay, well, we're going to learn something different."

Elements of Change at Greenfield Middle School

One of the more critical elements of transformation, according to Principal Bever, was working on changing the attitudes, opinions, and behaviors of the teaching staff. One structural change Bever implemented was the establishment of an executive committee, comprised of leaders from each of the middle school teams within the building, charged with much of the disciplinary decision making.

> We started asking our folks to think logically through the discipline piece. . . . The most severe thing we can do is separate a student from school. . . . This is punitive and not always effective in terms of the individual's education. We have to look at another way of doing it. . . . I'm really asking those team leaders [on the executive committee] to truly be leaders of the building. . . . They really assume a lot of the decision-making basis in the building.

Further, a strong emphasis was placed on responsible behavior and decision making among the teaching faculty.

> Walk your talk. When teachers don't model the behaviors they expect out of their students, the stage is set for disaster. And when you have teachers who rule through intimidation, you're going to have a mess in your school because the kids will respond similarly. . . . Kids must come first. Every decision we make at Greenfield Middle school always proceeds with the question "what is going to be best for the kids?"

Bever also believed it important to challenge assumptions that the students at Greenfield were "bad" students. Due to a recent redistricting process that redistributed many students in the school district, a commonly held belief among many was that Greenfield received the "worst" students. Bever believed it essential to challenge this belief:

> "The first task really involved getting them [teaching faculty] to see that our kids are not the worst students. Are they different maybe than some of the kids they had here before? Yes. Are they less able? Absolutely not."

To reinforce the notion that Greenfield's students were just as capable as the students who had been transferred during redistricting, Bever showed his teaching staff that the students at Greenfield had a cognitive aptitude score (as assessed by the state's mandatory accountability examination) that was within one point, plus or minus, of the students they had "lost."

Principal Bever also placed a heavy emphasis on collaborating with community agencies in transforming the disciplinary climate at Greenfield. Bever believed he had to take a swift and direct approach in getting a school with serious and at times violent behavior under control. In his words,

> The very first thing I did was to take a very aggressive approach to the discipline piece. I immediately began involving the local police department. We began hiring uniformed security for a lot of our after school functions. . . . So, the first thing I did was come in here with a real hard line effort.

In retrospect, however, Principal Bever indicated that this approach was necessary, but not an optimal long-term solution, in establishing safety at Greenfield. The purpose of using local law enforcement, according to Bever, was to establish safety, not to manage student behavior. It is thus not surprising that since safety has been established at Greenfield through a greater variety of disciplinary options, a uniformed police presence is no longer necessary. Interestingly, however, the ties between Greenfield and local law enforcement have not ceased but rather have been transformed into a more collaborative relationship.

> It's the same thing with the police department. . . . They get to see what we were about and what we stood for which was not taking troubled kids and getting them out the door. . . . We've really opened the door to them. We invite uniformed officers on shift to come in and eat with the kids. I have a detective on the police department who has become very, very involved in our parent leadership group. . . . They've come in and done defensive tactics training. . . . They have talks with our students about self protection and how to stay out of situations that could get them in trouble. . . . We have a wonderful relationship where we help them by not putting kids out on the street who are going to end up becoming a problem for them. We try to find alternatives.

The strategy of using external agencies to make Greenfield a safer and more responsive school has also been extended to agencies beyond law enforcement.

> I began to establish some good bridges to community organizations, the police department, the probation department, family social services, and child protective services. . . . We work a great deal with the probation department with attendance. . . . That's been a great thing. If I had a student in need or I have a student that I suspect may be involved in an abusive situation at home, one quick

call to child protective services and we get incredibly fast and cooperative responses
to respond collaboratively to support this student and get them through this difficult
time.

Outcomes of a Different Approach

The change in culture and climate at Greenfield has been dramatic according
to Principal Bever.

> We just don't see the issues of physical violence anymore. Do we have aggressive
> middle school boys in pushing and shoving matches now and then? Yes. Do we have
> the highly aggressive fist throwing and all-out fights? No. Very, very rarely does that
> happen anymore. The office referrals we now see are more typical with what you're
> going to see when dealing with middle schools.

Data drawn from the state of Indiana database on out-of-school suspension
and expulsion over the last eight years (Indiana Department of Education,
2004) provide additional evidence of the disciplinary changes at Greenfield.
Table 6.2 is a comparison of the disciplinary infractions for the year prior to
Bever's arrival and during the first year of his principalship. The out-of-
school suspension incident rate dropped from 50.67 incidents per 100 students in 1998–1999, to 18.53 incidents per 100 students in 1999–2000.
Moreover, the number of suspensions and expulsions for drugs, weapons, and
alcohol incidents dropped from fourteen to one, even with increases in student enrollment.

These changes in the data appear to be maintained over time. Comparing
the four years prior to Bever assuming the principalship to the four years of

Table 6.2   Disciplinary infractions at Greenfield Middle School: 1998–1999 and
1999–2000 School Years[a]

School Year	School Enrollment	OSS[b]	OSS Rate[c]	DWA[d]	DWA Rate[e]
1998–1999	450	228	50.67	14	3.11
1999–2000	475	88	18.53	1	0.21

Note: Jim Bever became principal during the 1999–2000 school year.
[a] Data were drawn from the Suspension and Expulsion Report form from the Indiana Department of Education.
[b] OSS is the total incidents of out-of-school suspension.
[c] OSS Rate is calculated by dividing the total number of out-of-school suspensions by the total school enrollment, multiplied by 100. Thus, this rate represents the total out-of-school suspension incidents per 100 students
and can be compared across school years.
[d] DWA (Drugs, Weapons, and Alcohol) is the total number of suspensions and expulsions for drugs, weapons,
and alcohol.
[e] DWA Rate is calculated by dividing the total number of suspensions and expulsions for drugs, weapons, and
alcohol by the total school enrollment, multiplied by 100. This rate represents the total drug, weapon, and
alcohol incidents per 100 students and can be compared across school years.

his tenure as principal, the out-of-school suspension and expulsion incident rates have dropped significantly (see figure 6.1) and, since 2000, are roughly equivalent to state averages for middle schools (Rausch and Skiba, 2004).

Further, the average numbers of suspensions and expulsions for drugs, weapons, and alcohol have dropped almost eightfold (see figure 6.2). Very clearly then, the different disciplinary approaches and philosophies taking hold at Greenfield Middle School have changed the consequences experienced by its students.

Importantly, these changes in disciplinary climate and outcome appear to extend to the learning environment. Bever notes that test scores have increased, although he still hopes for more improvement.

That piece [the learning environment] is much slower to respond. We are seeing a difference, however. Our teachers are learning how to retool their teaching to focus

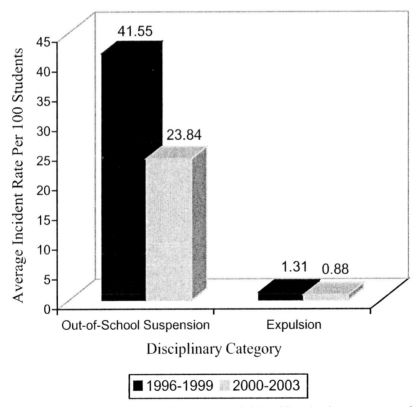

Figure 6.1. Disciplinary Incident Rates at Greenfield Middle School: 1996–1999 and 2000–2003 School Years

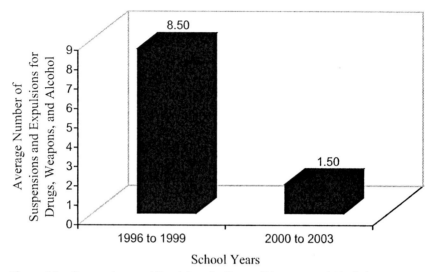

Figure 6.2.   Suspensions and Expulsions for Drugs, Weapons, and Alcohol at
Greenfield Middle School: 1996–1999 and 2000–2003

not on their teaching but rather [on] the students' learning. We've seen some appre-
ciable increases in student achievement over the past several years, but I don't think
that we're performing at a level that is consistent with our students' ability.

Bever attributes some of the gains in student learning to changes in the
teacher-student relationship: "What we do see though is just much more positive interactions between students and teachers, and I think that alone has
certainly helped us out in terms of the learning environment."

Bever may be underestimating the effects of school climate change and
improvements in student achievement at Greenfield Middle School. Figure
6.3 shows that since the 2000–2001 school year, one year after Bever became
principal, Greenfield Middle School's percentage of students passing both the
English/language arts and math sections of the state's accountability assessment has been higher than the state median for Indiana middle schools, aver-
aging around a sixty percent passing rate.

Principal Bever is quick to point out that he believes there is still much
work yet to be done at Greenfield, stating, "We're moving in the right direction, but again, I'll emphasize we're measuring in millimeters movement that
needs to be measured in miles." He is especially cognizant of the demands
placed on staff by a more preventive and individualized approach to school
discipline.

Every move we make creates a ripple, in effect, placing increasing demands on our
faculty. Innovation and improvement puts a great deal of pressure on our staff to

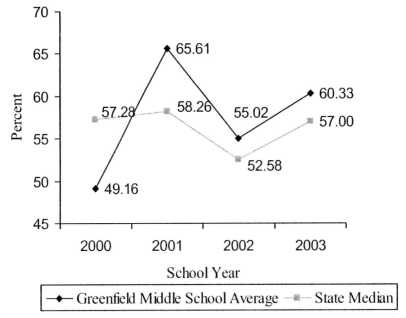

Figure 6.3. Percent of Students Passing State Accountability Examination at Greenfield Middle School Compared to State Median for All Middle Schools

learn new things and conduct business differently, all the while continuing to work with up to 170 students per day. We've done a lot of good on very, very few resources. It's taxing, and our folks are really spread far too thin.

He feels strongly that policymakers must be aware of the resources that schools need in order to develop more effective disciplinary climates. In particular, he argues for state resources to support the presence of more adult role models.

Only 15 percent of a youngster's time, from kindergarten through the senior year of high school, is spent under the direct influence of the school and its personnel. Even though that is relatively little time, we can have a significant positive impact on our students if we play our game reasonably well. I need additional high quality, well prepared adults who can work with kids in small ratios. In this manner, we can maximize the impact of good, adult role models on our students' lives.

CONCLUSIONS

Every day, principals are faced with the complex job of bringing hundreds of students from widely varying backgrounds together and ensuring that they can focus on their schoolwork, not disruptions. The principals described in this paper have sought and found methods that allow them to preserve the safety and integrity of the learning climate in their schools while maximizing student opportunity to learn. While zero tolerance school discipline may currently be popular among many educational administrators and political leaders, the principals we interviewed described many alternatives to student removal, suggesting that exclusionary disciplinary systems are not the only way of ensuring school safety and productivity.

To be sure, these principals made it clear that there are students who threaten the safety of the learning environment and who need to be removed from the school environment for a period of time. Yet, they also used practices and approaches seeking to prevent negative behavior from occurring, they focused on establishing meaningful relationships with disconnected students, and they sought to implement creative alternatives to exclusion for students engaged in disruptive and even severe behavior. These perspectives are congruent with national research documenting the effectiveness of preventive planning and implementation (Dwyer et al., 1998; Elliott et al., 2001; Gagnon and Leone, 2001; Mihalic et al., 2001; Skiba et al., forthcoming; Thornton et al., 2000).

Student attitude and behavior contribute to the likelihood of being removed from school (Wu et al., 1982). Yet, differences in beliefs and practices among educators that relate to different outcomes for students suggests that the choices made by educators, principals in particular, substantially contribute to student exclusion (Bowditch, 1993; Dunbar and Villarruel, 2004; Mukuria, 2004; Raffaele Mendez et al., 2002; Vavrus and Cole, 2002; Wu et al., 1982). Thus, the fact that some principals, even those serving "tough" student populations (Mukuria, 2004; Raffaele Mendez et al., 2002), are able to maintain the integrity of the learning environment without removing large numbers of students from the opportunity to learn illustrates that there are efficacious alternatives to student removal.

The implementation of different ways of disciplining students is not resource-free. In an era when schools and teachers are being required to do more and more with fewer resources, placing the responsibility of change solely on the backs of educators can be overwhelming to those personnel. A substantial commitment of time, effort, and scarce school resources has been necessary to create the changes seen at Greenfield Middle School and other schools (Raffaele Mendez et al., 2002; Richart et al., 2004). This suggests that provisions of additional targeted resources are necessary for these preventive approaches to take hold, grow, and evolve.

Even with limited resources, however, the principals highlighted in this paper have sought and found methods that allow them to preserve the safety and integrity of the learning climate in their schools without removing large numbers of students from the opportunity to learn. Their perspectives, programs, and practices serve as models for school and community leaders interested in ensuring safe and effective schools for all students. As our knowledge of available options for promoting a safe and effective school climate increases, it becomes apparent that there is no contradiction between the need to keep schools safe and the mandate to maximize educational opportunity for all children.

NOTES

1. Further information on the Children Left Behind project, including briefing papers and supplemental analyses, can be found at the project website, ceep.indiana.edu/ChildrenLeftBehind.

2. For the complete study, see Skiba, Rausch, and Ritter (2004), *"Discipline is Always Teaching": Effective Alternatives to Zero Tolerance in Indiana's Schools*, ceep.indiana.edu/ChildrenLeftBehind.

3. For more detail, see Rausch and Skiba (2004), *Doing Discipline Differently: The Greenfield Middle School Story*, ceep.indiana.edu/ChildrenLeftBehind.

REFERENCES

Advancement Project. (2005). *Education on Lockdown: The Schoolhouse to Jailhouse Track*. Washington, DC: Author.

Ayers, W., Dohrn, B., and Ayers, R. (2001). *Zero Tolerance: Resisting the Drive for Punishment in Our Schools*. New York: The New Press.

Bickel, F., and Qualls, R. (1980). The impact of school climate on suspension rates in the Jefferson County public schools. *Urban Review 12*, 79–86.

Bowditch, C. (1993). Getting rid of troublemakers: High school disciplinary procedures and the production of dropouts. *Social Problems 40*, 493–507.

Davis, J. E., and Jordan, W. J. (1994). The effects of school context, structure, and experiences on African American males in middle and high schools. *Journal of Negro Education 63*, 570–587.

Dunbar, C., and Villarruel, F. A. (2004). What a difference the community makes: Zero tolerance policy interpretation and implementation. *Equity and Excellence in Education 37*, 351–359.

Dwyer, K., Osher, D., and Warger, C. (1998). *Early Warning, Timely Response: A Guide to Safe Schools*. Washington, DC: U.S. Department of Education.

Elliott, D. S., Hamburg, B. A., and Williams, K. R. (1998). *Violence in American Schools*. Cambridge, UK: Cambridge University Press.

Elliott, D., Hatot, N. J., Sirovatka, P., and Potter, B. B. (2001). *Youth Violence: A Report of the Surgeon General*. Washington, DC: U.S. Surgeon General.

Gagnon, J. C., and Leone, P. E. (2001). Alternative strategies for youth violence prevention. In R. J. Skiba and G. G. Noam (eds.), *New Directions for Youth Development* (no. 92; Zero tolerance: Can suspension and expulsion keep school safe? pp. 101–125). San Francisco: Jossey-Bass.

Gordon, R., Della Piana, L., and Keleher, T. (2001). *Facing the Consequences: An Examination of Racial Discrimination in U.S. Public Schools.* Oakland, CA: Applied Research Center.

Harvard Civil Rights Conference. (2000, February). *Opportunities Suspended: The Devastating Consequences of Zero Tolerance and School Discipline.* Cambridge, MA: Author.

Herald Times. (2001, December 12). Report of gun threat nets arrest of boy, 15. *The Herald Times*, Bloomington, IN.

Indiana Department of Education. (2004). *K–12 School Data.* Available at www.doe.state .in.us.

Mansfield, W., and Farris, E. (1992). *Office for Civil Rights Survey Redesign: A Feasibility Study.* Rockville, MD: Westat, Inc.

Michigan Public Policy Initiative. (2003). *Zero Tolerance Policies and Their Impact on Michigan Students.* Available at www.mnaonline.org/pdf/spotlight%202002_12.pdf.

Mihalic, S., Irwin, K., Elliott, D., Fagan, A., and Hansen, D. (2001, July). *Blueprints for Violence Prevention* (OJJDP Juvenile Justice Bulletin). Washington, DC: U.S. Department of Justice, Office of Juvenile Justice and Delinquency Prevention.

Morrison, G. M., Morrison, R. L., and Minjarez, M. E. (1999). Student pathways through school discipline options: system and individual interactions. Paper presented at the 23rd Annual Conference on Severe Behavior Disorders of Children and Youth, Scottsdale, AZ.

Mukuria, G. (2002). Disciplinary challenges: How do principals address this dilemma? *Urban Education 37*, 432–452.

Noguera, P. A. (1995). Preventing and producing violence: A critical analysis of responses to school violence. *Harvard Educational Review 65*, 189–212.

Potts, K., Njie, B., Detch, E. R., and Walton, J. (2003). *Zero Tolerance in Tennessee Schools: An Update* (ERIC ED481971). Nashville, TN: Office of Education Accountability, State of Tennessee.

Public Law 103-227. (1994). Gun-Free Schools Act. SEC 1031, 20 USC 2701.

Public Law 107-110. (2002). The No Child Left Behind Act of 2001. 20 USC 6301.

Raffaele Mendez, L. M., Knoff, H. M., and Ferron, J. F. (2002). School demographic variables and out-of-school suspension rates: A quantitative and qualitative analysis of a large, ethnically diverse school district. *Psychology in the Schools 39*, 259–277.

Rausch, M. K., and Skiba, R. J. (2004). *Doing Discipline Differently: The Greenfield Middle School Story.* Bloomington, IN: Center for Evaluation and Education Policy. Available at ceep.indiana.edu/ChildrenLeftBehind.

Rausch, M. K., Skiba, R. J., and Simmons, A. B. (2005, April). The academic cost of discipline: School disciplines contribution to achievement. Paper presented at the American Educational Research Association Conference, Montreal, Canada.

Richart, D., Brooks, K., and Soler, M. (2003). *Unintended Consequences: The Impact of Zero Tolerance and Other Exclusionary Policies on Kentucky's Students.* Washington, DC: Building Blocks for Youth.

Richart, D., Soler, M., Spurlock, S., Scantlebury, J., and Brooks Tandy, K. (2004). *North-*

ern Lights: Success in Student Achievement and School Discipline at Northern Elementary School. Washington, DC: Building Blocks for Youth.

Rose, T. L. (1988). Current disciplinary practices with handicapped students: Suspensions and expulsions. *Exceptional Children 55*, 230–239.

Silverman, D. (2000). *Doing Qualitative Research: A Practical Handbook*. Thousand Oakes, CA: SAGE Publications.

Skiba, R. J. (2004). *Zero Tolerance: The Assumptions and the Facts*. Bloomington, IN: Center for Evaluation and Education Policy. Available at ceep.indiana.edu/Children LeftBehind.

Skiba, R. J., and Edl, H. (2004). *The Disciplinary Practices Survey: How Do Indiana's Principals Feel about Discipline?* Bloomington, IN: Center for Evaluation and Education Policy. Available at ceep.indiana.edu/ChildrenLeftBehind.

Skiba, R. J., Michael, R. S., Nardo, A. C., and Peterson, R. (2002). The color of discipline: Sources of racial and gender disproportionality in school punishment. *Urban Review 34*, 317–342.

Skiba, R. J., and Peterson, R. L. (1999). The dark side of zero tolerance: Can punishment lead to safe schools? *Phi Delta Kappan 80*, 372–376, 381–382.

Skiba, R. J, Peterson, R., Miller, C., Ritter, S., and Simmons, A. (forthcoming). The safe and responsive schools project: A school reform model for implementing best practices in violence prevention. In S. Jimerson and M. Furlong (eds.), *Handbook of School Violence and School Safety*. Mahwah, NJ: Lawrence Erlbaum Associates

Skiba, R. J., Peterson, R. L., and Williams, T. (1997). Office referrals and suspension: Disciplinary intervention in middle schools. *Education and Treatment of Children 20*, 295–315.

Skiba, R. J, Rausch, M. K., and Ritter, S. (2004). *"Discipline is Always Teaching": Effective Alternatives to Zero Tolerance in Indiana's Schools*. Bloomington, IN: Center for Evaluation and Education Policy. Available at ceep.indiana.edu/ChildrenLeftBehind.

Thornton, T. N., Craft, C. A., Dahlberg, L. L., Lynch, B. S., and Baer, K. (2000). *Best Practices of Youth Violence Prevention: A Sourcebook for Community Action*. Atlanta: Centers for Disease Control and Prevention, National Center for Injury Prevention and Control.

Tobin, T., Sugai, G., and Colvin, G. (1996). Patterns in middle school discipline records. *Journal of Emotional and Behavioral Disorders 4*, 82–94.

Uchitelle, S., Bartz, D., and Hillman, L. (1989). Strategies for reducing suspensions. *Urban Education 24*, 163–176.

U.S. Department of Education. (2000). *The 2000–2001 Elementary and Secondary School Survey: National and State Projections*. Washington, DC: U.S. Government Printing Office. Available at 205.207.175.84/ocr2000r/wdsdata.html.

Vavrus, F., and Cole, K. (2002). "I didn't do nothin'": The discursive construction of school suspension. *The Urban Review 34*, 87–111.

Verdugo, R. (2002). Race-ethnicity, social class, and zero tolerance policies: The cultural and structural wars. *Education and Urban Society 35*, 50–75.

Vossekuil, B., Fein, R. A., Reddy, M., Borum, R., and Modzeleski, W. (2002). *The Final Report and Findings of the Safe School Initiative: Implications for the Prevention of School Attacks in the United States*. Washington, DC: United States Secret Service and United States Department of Education.

Wald, J., and Losen, D. J. (2003). Defining and redirecting a school-to-prison pipeline. In J. Wald and D. J. Losen (eds.), *New Directions for Youth Development* (no. 99; Deconstructing the school-to-prison pipeline, pp. 9–15). San Francisco: Jossey-Bass.

Wu, S. C., Pink, W. T., Crain, R. L., and Moles, O. (1982). Student suspension: A critical reappraisal. *The Urban Review 14*, 245–303.

Yin, R. K. (2003). *Case Study Research: Design and Methods*. 3rd ed. Thousand Oakes, CA: SAGE Publications.

7

Recommendations and Conclusions

Zero tolerance policies provide two distinct policy tracks. The first track is defined by the Gun-Free Schools Act of 1994. It prohibits guns, drugs, tobacco, and other weapons in or near schools. This law requires that students be suspended or expelled from school. The policy, as it was written and intended, protects students and teachers and makes public schools more secure; it was intended as good policy for safe school environments. Principals must make every effort to prevent crime in the school so that schools are safe havens.

It is the thoughtlessness with which many zero tolerance policies are implemented that has created conflicts. Knives are weapons, and drugs are illegal and grounds for removal. No consideration was given when a butter knife was accidentally left in a vehicle or a fingernail file was left in a purse. Midol, aspirins, cough drops, and asthma pumps morphed into prohibited drugs. Over time, many of these discrepancies have been corrected. The student removal data from Texas show that only five percent of all the student discipline infractions in the state of Texas are for the mandatory zero tolerance infractions as identified by federal and state law.

The second track of zero tolerance policies poses major concerns. These are state and local policies that emerged or evolved from federal legislation, defined in state policy as discretionary policies, which in Texas represent approximately 95 percent of all disciplinary infractions. The second phase of zero tolerance policies threatens equal educational opportunity, school desegregation, and equitable resources. National and state school suspension and expulsion data show that second phase zero tolerance adversely affects minority, low-income, special education, and male students. The theories upon which zero tolerance policies are grounded suggest a substantive shift in American education policy. No longer is universal, free public education a policy for minority and low-income students. The Texas DAEP grade level enrollment reported that African American students in the first to fifth grade made up more than twice as many DAEP enrollments as their state enrollment for those grade levels. African American students made up 14 percent of the first through sixth grade-level state enrollment but they made up 37 percent of the DAEP placements. Elementary school socializes students into the educational system and the school environment. When students are removed at the high rates that African American and Hispanic students are removed in the elementary level, some theoretical assumptions provide conclusions for the data.

Zero tolerance policies are grounded in law and order theory and have criminalized the education process. Law and order theory specifies that the state has full responsibility for establishing the guilt and punishment of those who break the law (Mantle, Fox, and Dhami, 2003). One of the requirements of the Gun-Free Schools Act was that school districts coordinate with the local law enforcement office of the county juvenile office. The second phase of zero tolerance policies outlawed school disruptions by classifying them as class C misdemeanors. The purpose of law and order theory is to punish the offenders or those who break the law, to use harsh punishment as a deterrent from future misconduct, and to separate offenders from the community. School discipline policy requires that students be punished even for minor infractions. Based on the discipline infraction level, harsh punishment increases. Under this theory, sending students to court deters future discipline infractions. Students who misbehave need to be isolated in separate facilities, like DAEPs and JJAEPs. The punishment will result in a decrease in discipline infractions. The punishment for breaking the rules is tough, without any considerations.

Law and order theory also purports to be color blind. It recognizes that all are equal before the law and those who break the law deserve to be punished. If minority, low-income, and special education students break discipline rules, they deserve to be removed from school without any consideration for circumstances or context. Sociological and psychological issues should not be a consideration in education (Lazear, 2002). Law and order theory is about using punishment to teach a moral lesson while serving as a deterrent to crime. Law and order theory protects traditional values. Zero tolerance is about using punishment to teach moral lessons. It is not about teaching appropriate behavior or behavioral expectations.

In the case of overrepresentation of African American and Latino students in elementary DAEP placements, the moral lessons to be taught by zero tolerance policies are that parents need to send children to school, ready to listen and learn. Children in the elementary grades should have traditional social skills and academic preparation to learn, such as reliability, loyalty, and capacity to take directions. If children are able to sit quietly and listen to the teacher, they will learn. The assumption is that learning is an absorption process that occurs from passively sitting and listening. Children should come to school with the right work and discipline ethic (Lazear, 2002). Disruptive misbehavior denies an education to those students who want to learn. "Too many students are losing critical opportunities for learning—and too many teachers are leaving the profession—because of the behavior of a few persistent troublemakers" (Public Agenda, 2004). There is a surface lure to these no-nonsense assumptions.

The danger of moral lessons in zero tolerance is that education is no longer universal. Under this approach, only those who deserve an education are entitled to one. If minorities, low-income, and special education students are overrepresented in suspensions, expulsions, DAEPs, and JJAEPs, it is because they do not come to school with the right work and discipline ethic. The goal of education reform is to produce high test scores. Addressing the needs of disadvantaged students only detracts from producing higher test scores (Lazear, 2002). These are all alarming conclusions with major policy implications.

The Texas data reviewed in chapters 2 and 3 show the ineffectiveness of zero tolerance in one state. Rather than serving as a deterrent to student misbehavior, in most categories, disciplinary infractions increased at a greater rate than the rate the state student enrollment increased. In discipline categories that showed some decreases over the six-year period, the recidivism rate increased. Achievement data as measured by state accountability scores and SAT1 scores decreased slightly. SAT1 scores were also lower than were the national means. It would be simplistic to conclude that the state's zero tolerance produced lower achievement. However, one has to ask, what effect did zero tolerance have on achievement?

The research and the literature provide evidence that practitioners are questioning the effectiveness of zero tolerance policies. School districts have made enormous investments in security equipment when the evidence shows that most schools remain safe environments (U.S. Department of Education, 2005; Verdugo, 2005). Most principals have recognized the need to move beyond metal detectors to prevent violent crime while increasing student achievement.

Rausch and Skiba from the Indiana University Center for Evaluation and Policy Education conducted a study focusing on the perspectives and practices of school leaders in one midwestern state. They found that the philosophy and practice of zero tolerance school discipline has failed as an educational intervention to ensure student safety, improve school climates, advance student learning, or provide equitable results; yet, the approach remains popular among many educational administrators and political leaders. The popularity of zero tolerance, however, does not mean that all educational leaders subscribe to this paradigm. Absent from much of the research base to date are the voices of teachers and school principals actively promoting alternative philosophies and practices better suited to meet the paramount goals of student safety and learning.

Teachers in the United States remain divided on zero tolerance policies. The National Education Association and the American Federation of Teachers supported zero tolerance at its inception. NEA supports educationally sound zero tolerance and a bill of rights for children. NEA supports a policy that "consists of a set of child-centered, reasonable, and nonpunitive sanctions that make clear to all students, parents, school employees, and community agencies that certain kinds of student behavior are not welcomed on or around school grounds" (Verdugo, 2005, 15).

Chapter 5 reports the findings from a series of focus groups conducted with five cohorts of middle and high school teachers in New England. Some teachers reported their frustration with inconsistent administrators who failed to communicate one clear and consistent policy and failed to support teachers. Consequently, this led to unfair treatment of students and usurping of teacher authority. In large secondary schools, the large numbers of school administrators blurred consistent implementation of policies. Other teachers reported a well-communicated discipline philosophy and policy. While teachers did not report a fear of violence, they did feel worn down by petty spats, verbal abuse, offensive language, dress code violations, and minor altercations between students. Teachers were frustrated that discipline policies did not offer options to ineffective suspensions. Suspension only led to repeat offenses and did not change behavior. They expressed concerns that removing the student from the school or referring students to local law enforcement only worsened the conditions for students. The use of zero tolerance policies creates a system of student misdiagnosis. When students are randomly suspended or expelled for all misbehavior, students who really need counseling resources or evaluation for special services become the victims of misdiagnosis. After three misdiagnosed removals, the students predictably lose interest in school. Teachers expressed the desire for counseling, social services, and other services provided by full-service schools. One teacher recommended using a triage system similar to what schools recommend.

Teacher focus groups expressed the need for administrators to regularly and consistently communicate discipline policies to teachers, students, and staff. They expressed a desire for more creative and varied discipline options with support programs. Teachers would rather eliminate dress codes than consistently remove students for dress code violations. They would like to have more counseling and other services for students in the place of suspending students. Finally, teachers recognize that they need more classroom management training.

Chapter 6 describes the findings of a survey conducted with 324 principals in the Midwest. The survey focused on the perspectives and practices of school leaders in one midwestern state. The emerging results of this project suggest that (1) diversity exists among school principals in their endorsement of zero tolerance school discipline, (2) the disciplinary perspectives of school principals is related to the use of exclusionary student removal and the use of preventive alternatives, and (3) the perspective of principals endorsing alternatives to student exclusion suggests that removing students from the learning environment is not the only method available for keeping students safe to learn.

Principals reported three perspectives on school discipline. The first perspective is from principals who used preventive interventions, working closely with parents and providing several student support programs to build expected student behavioral skills. A second group of principals reported using student suspensions and expulsions to control discipline and compensate for uninvolved parents. Principals were too busy to develop personal relationships with students. The third group used pragmatic prevention but did not rule out student removals; however, this group, like the first group, provided student support and mentoring programs to build student behavioral skills.

The second part of the principal study conducted interviews with a group of principals. Principals reported the use of consistent communication with the faculty and staff to develop a common understanding of the campus discipline program. The principal focused on working closely with parents. Students who posed a higher school disruption risk were targeted for building close and trusting relationships. Principals were clear that they would not put up with misbehavior. Principals reported that it was important to understand the relationship between achievement and behavior.

Zero tolerance policies that remove students from school often only contribute to student failure. Recommendations for alternatives to zero tolerance removals are common sense. These recommendations were found in the leadership activities of principals who used alternatives to suspension. They were also evident in alternatives identified by the teacher focus groups.

CLASSROOM MANAGEMENT

Issues of school violence and student misbehavior will not be solved with a magic pill or a magic program. They will take a combination of programs, services, attitude, knowledge, and skills for the leadership of school principals. Mandatory zero tolerance policies set the foundation for a safe school environment. Safe schools and reasonable implementation of mandatory school removals remain a priority for school principals. School leaders must define, support, and maintain high standards for behavior and achievement. Research shows that improved school organization can reduce overall student disruption (Freiberg, Prokosch, Treister, & Stein, 1990; Gottfredson, 1986; Gottfredson et al., 1993).

Discretionary student removals make up approximately 95 percent of all student removals. There are concerns about the overrepresentation of minority and low-income students in student removals from school. Some school administrators and teachers have found alternative solutions to address discipline problems, reduce class disruptions, and increase achievement.

Teachers will continue to be the frontline managers for student discipline. If student behavior is to change, teachers will be responsible for that change (Grossman, 2004). It will take a multitude of classroom management techniques to change student behavior. The foundation for reducing student classroom disruptions is a highly skilled adult with the knowledge, skills, and ability to manage the classroom (Freiberg, 1999). Brophy (1988) defines classroom management as "the actions taken to create and maintain a learning environment conducive to attainment of the goals of instruction—arranging the physical environment of the classroom, establishing rules and procedures, maintaining attention to lessons and engagement in academic activities" (2). Classroom management is synonymous with discipline, yet most new teachers entering teaching in the last ten years have received virtually no development for classroom management. Alternative certified teachers receive minimum preparation and study few, if any, classroom management methods and skills development. Many teacher certification programs have omitted classroom management from the teacher preparation curriculum. New teachers are minimally prepared to manage students.

Research shows that the primary reason teachers leave teaching is because they lack classroom management and student discipline skills (Brophy, 1999; McCaslin and Good, 1992; Patterson, Roehrig, and Luff, 2003). The research shows the connections between classroom management, student behavior, and achievement (Freiberg, Connell, and Lorentz, 2001). Classroom management has been identified as one in a list of five variables that influence school learning (Wang, Haertel and Walberg, 1993).

Fairness and teacher attitude are crucial to students. Disruptive behavior is symptomatic of school and societal problems that influence teachers and students. When students break class or school rules, teachers and administrators often treat students differently based on income and race (Brantlinger, 1993; Irvine, 1991). Children who are treated differently because they come from lower-income families are subjected to unjust learning environments. Even the youngest child recognizes when a teacher is not fair. Consequently, low-income students may behave more aggressively. The data in chapter 2 show that 60 to 70 percent of school removals are low-income students.

Classroom management can be undermined by policies that demand simple, unreflective obedience (McCaslin and Good, 1992). Students respond more positively in classroom climates that are grounded in care, fairness, and connectedness. When students feel connected and feel that they are cared for by people in the school, they are less likely to use substances, engage in violence, or act out (McNeely, Nonnemaker and Blum, 2002). One of the lessons learned from Columbine is that violent students tell someone before they commit a violent act. The most effective violence prevention tool in schools has been relationships and trust between students and teachers and students and administrators (Joiner, 2002). Many major violent episodes across the country have been prevented since Columbine by other students who reported crime plans to teachers or school administrators. One study reported that after one year, a classroom management program that promotes connectedness and self-discipline reduced the number of students sent to the office by 30 to 100 percent.

Connectedness is important at all grade levels, starting in the first grade. One study found that peer rejection in the first or second grade produced third-grade aggression scores that were five times higher for students who were rejected by their peers in lower grades (Dodge et al., 2003). The study concludes that lack of opportunity for social interaction and positive peer group may inhabit social development and self-discipline. For example, in data for Texas grade-level DAEP placements, African American placements peaked in the third grade (table 3.1). While they were disproportionately placed in the DAEP at every grade level, the highest number of placements was in the first, second, and third grade. The theory suggests that teacher understanding of student connectedness as a classroom management strategy would decrease the number of elementary school removals for African American students. The teacher's ability to produce a classroom environment that promotes social interactions and positive peer group relations would also increase African American student well-being and reduce removals from the classroom; it would follow that this strategy would work for all students.

Classroom management prepares teachers for the diversity of U.S. schools

(Freiberg, Prokosch, Treister, & Stein, 1990). Teachers need classroom management techniques that expose them to the developmental needs and information on diverse student populations, including racial, ethnic, linguistic, income, and gender. Classroom management provides an understanding of the impact that gender differences, sexual identify, ethnicity, income status, transience, migration, immigration, culture, language, and child abuse have on classroom behavior (Grossman, 2004).

In addition to classroom management, teachers need development in behavior management and instructional strategies for students with disabilities and different learning needs. The Individuals with Disabilities Education Act (IDEA) requires that states ensure that teachers receive appropriate and adequate training to meet the learning needs of special needs students. The Texas data showed that while special education students made up 12 percent of the state disabilities populations, they made up approximately 23 percent of all student removals, twice their rate of enrollment.

ALTERNATIVE DISCIPLINE SYSTEMS

Alternative discipline systems like the graduated system have reported drastic reductions in school suspensions. Graduated discipline systems reserve the most severe consequences for the worst offenses. Troubled students are counseled to help them cope better with bullying and conflict. As one example, a graduated discipline system in Clearwater High School in Florida cut suspension rates by 65 percent over four years. The school's dropout rate and frequency of classroom disruptions also decreased while test scores increased (Mendez, 2003).

The Texas data showed that while the number of students removed from school was decreasing, recidivism was increasing. Judges in chapter 4 reported that many of the students who were ticketed for student disruptions were in need of counseling, testing, social services, and literacy development. No support services or interventions were provided by the schools. Mendez (2003) recommends a three-stage model for preventing violence in schools. By addressing the problems of discipline rather than temporarily removing them, behavior recidivism is reduced. The first step of the model recommends that schools build a schoolwide foundation that includes students' needs through a positive school climate and support services for students and their families. The second recommends an early intervention by creating support and services for students at risk for serious academic or behavioral problems. The final step recommends that schools provide intensive interventions that are coordinated, sustained, and culturally appropriate for students with demonstrated needs (Osher, Sandler, and Nelson, 2001). The Osher, Sandler, and Nelson model is a useful framework for any student behavior and discipline plan.

Another prevention strategy is to reduce the size of large high schools. Large, overcrowded high schools have created large communities where students do not get personal attention, fall behind, and become alienated. Building small learning communities have allowed large, overcrowded urban high schools to develop personalized learning communities. As an example, Patterson High School in Baltimore created five small academies using a career-focused curriculum and personalized instruction. The small communities allowed teachers to have more interaction with the same students over four years. The personalized attention dramatically improved student behavior, attendance, and achievement (McPartland et al., 1997).

SCHOOL COUNSELORS: A PREVENTION STRATEGY

The need for counseling services are evident throughout this book. It took Judge Johanna less than five minutes with students to assess the need for counseling and testing services. The judge, with the help of a social worker assigned to her court, was able to identify counseling resources for students. While she was able to refer students to counseling services, she also acknowledged that community counseling and social services were scarce. Teachers recognize that they do not have the time to provide one-to-one counseling. They have even less time to provide social and emotional skill development. Teachers, principals, and judges identified the need for counseling services for students with behavioral problems; however, counselors in public schools find themselves with huge student loads, increasing testing responsibilities, and shrinking resources. According to the American School Counselor Association (2005), the national counselor-to-student average is 478 to 1. In California, the ratio is 951 to 1, in Texas it's 451 to 1, and in Massachusetts it's 336 to 1. Rather than building separate schools for students who break school rules, a systems approach to school improvement and reduction in school discipline infractions would increase the number of counselors. School counselors would interact directly with students before they are sent to court or removed to separate schools.

DISCIPLINARY ALTERNATIVE EDUCATION PROGRAMS (DAEP)

The research on alternative schools reports that there are forty-eight states with alternative schools legislation (Lehr, Lanners, and Lange, 2003). While there is no clear definition of what constitutes alternative school, there is practice to guide a definition. The Lehr, Lanners, and Lange study cautioned that alternative schools could have many purposes. States reported using more than one type of alternative school. For example, Texas reported using alternative schools that are schools of choice, DAEPs that are schools for mandatory placements, and JJAEPs that are schools for mandatory placements by the courts.

In addition to practice, there is theory to drive the definition of alternative schools. Raywid (1994) developed a model for defining alternative schools based on three types of schools. Type I includes innovative programs of choice. Type II utilizes disciplinary programs with mandatory placements. Type III is a developmental or therapeutic program that provides academic and discipline support to students. Of the three types, type I is the more desirable model, focusing on student needs using individualized instruction. The type I model assumes that something is wrong with an instructional program that does not meet the needs of the student.

The type I alternative school builds an instructional program around the learning needs of the student. For example, the Gonzalo Garza School of Independence in Texas has an enrollment of 400 students. The school operates on a morning schedule and an afternoon schedule to meet the needs of students who work or students who have family responsibilities. The school uses small-sized traditional classes, but they also use one-to-one instruction and computer-based instruction. Garza students are required to apply and interview for admissions. While there are no extracurricular activities, students find instructionally related activities that keep them on campus until late in the day. A substantial number of Garza students graduate and go on to college. Schools like Garza provide students who would drop out of school a last chance to graduate from high school. The per-pupil cost is equal to the public high school cost or less when consideration is given to the amount Garza saves the Austin Independent School District by properly educating high-cost, learning disabled, low-income, and at-risk students. The research shows that type I alternative schools are the most efficient and effective alternative schools.

The type II punitive model is a deficit school model. It is a school for mandatory placements. Nationally, 65 percent of all alternative schools use the type II model (Lehr and Lange 2003). Type II alternative schools are the model for DAEPs. In Texas, teachers were uncertified until 2006. The early attractions of DAEPs included using less qualified noncertified teachers and a minimal curriculum (Reyes, 2003). Nationally, DAEP accountability and curriculum have been reported as concerns. In Texas, DAEPs are primarily receiving schools when students are referred for discipline infractions. This was the warehouse type of program unsuccessfully challenged by Timothy Nevarez. According to Texas transfer policies, when a student transfers, the receiving schools does not have to report the student's accountability test scores. The scores go into the district average. Accountability is minimal for type II schools. In a study conducted by the University of Minnesota (2003), survey data for 48 states showed that type II schools lacked clearly-documented measures of effectiveness and student success or student outcomes (Lehr and Lange, 2003).

The research on alternative schools shows that type I alternative schools are more effective, efficient, and accountable than are type II schools used as DAEPs. The Texas DAEP grade-level data suggest that many minority students are placed in DAEPs for misbehavior when their real needs may be related to social skills, emotional skills, and literacy. A better policy than placing them in low-level punitive schools would be a facility that addressed their learning needs. When discretionary DAEP student disciplinary referrals are made, an admissions process that evaluates students' social skills, emotional skills, and academic needs should be mandatory. The evaluation process would be used to place students in DAEPs modeled on the type I model. These schools would cost no more than the punitive type II models. Mandatory DAEP referrals would be placed in the type II model. Texas data show that approximately 25 percent of all DAEP placements are for special education students. JJAEPs would exclusively serve court-appointed students and other students awaiting trial for a violent crime. Any JJAEP placements other than court appointments would require an assessment, review, and dismissal process with an individualized education plan. JJAEP referrals should be reserved for genuine problem cases not just for "continuous misbehavior."

CONCLUSIONS

In the future, school safety will continue to be an important function that school principals will perform. Protecting the safety of students and teachers must be the goal of any school discipline plan. However, zero tolerance mandatory policies should be fairly and consistently enforced. The punishment must fit the infraction. Schools cannot continue to send poor students to municipal, county, or state courts because they cannot afford a school uniform or because a student is caught in the middle of a divorce. School discipline plans need to be grounded in schoolwide efforts that support needs through a positive school climate and support services for students and their families. Student support should be provided with early intervention by creating support and services for students at risk for serious academic or behavioral problems. Intensive interventions should be coordinated, sustained, and culturally appropriate with the students' demonstrated needs.

The continued use of police-like zero tolerance policies to address 95 percent of the student removals for discretionary reasons poses threats to equal educational opportunity, school desegregation, and equitable resources. When students are removed from school because some families have not prepared them for the school's social environment, because they speak a different language, because they are poor, or because they have a learning disability, the right to a free, public education no longer exists. When this happens, as appears too often, all of us suffer.

REFERENCE

American School Counselors Association. (2005). Student to counselor ratio, www.schoolcounselor.org.

Brantlinger, E. (1993). Adolescent's interpretation of social class influences on schooling. *Journal of Classroom Interaction 28*(1), 1–12.

Brophy, J. (1988). Educating teachers about managing classrooms and students. *Teaching and Teacher Education 4*(1), 1–18.

Brophy, J. (1999). Perspectives of classroom management: Yesterday, today, and tomorrow. In H. J. Freiberg (ed.), *Beyond Behaviorism* (pp. 44–45). Needham Heights, MA: Allyn and Bacon.

Dodge, K. A., Lansford, J. E., Burks, V. S. Bates, J. E., Petit, G. S., Fountaine, R., and Price, J. M. (2003). Peer rejection and social information-processing factors in the development of aggressive behavior problems in children. *Child Development 74*(2), 374–393.

Freiberg, H. J. (1999). *Beyond Behaviorism: Changing the Classroom Management Paradigm.* Needham Heights, MA: Allyn & Bacon.

Freiberg, H. J., Prokosch, N., Treister, E. S., & Stein, T. A. (1990). Turning around five at-risk elementary schools. *Journal of School Effectiveness and School Improvement 1*, 5–25.

Freiberg, H. J., Connell, M. L., and Lorentz, J. (2001). Effects of consistency management on student mathematics achievement in seven chapter 1 elementary schools. *Journal of Education for Students Placed at Risk 6*(3), 249–270.

Gottfredson, D. (1986). Promising strategies for improving student behavior. Paper presented on Student Discipline Strategies of the Office of Educational Research and Improvement. U.S. Department of Education, Washington, DC.

Gottfredson, D., Gottfredson, G. D., and Hybl, L. G. (1993). Managing adolescent behavior: A multi-year, multi-school study. *American Educational Research Journal 30*(1), 179–215.

Grossman, H. (2004). *Classroom Behavior Management for Diverse and Inclusive Schools.* New York: Rowman & Littlefield.

Irvine, J. J. (1991). *Black Students and School Failure. Policies, Practices, and Prescriptions.* Westport, CT: Greenwood Press Inc.

Joiner, L. L. (2002). Life-saving lessons. *American School Board Journal 189*(3).

Lehr, C. A., and Lange, C. M. (2003). Alternative schools and the students they serve: Perceptions of state directors of special education. *Policy Research Brief 14*(1).

Lehr, C. A., Lanners, F. J., and Lange, C. M. (2003). Alternative schools: Policy and legislation across the United States. *Policy Research Brief 14*(1).

Lezear, E., ed. (2002). *Education in the Twenty-First Century.* Stanford, CA: Hoover Institution.

Mantle, M., Fox, D., and Dhami, M. K. (2003). Restorative justice and three individual theories of crime. *Internet Journal of Criminology.* Retrieved August 6, 2005, from www.internetjournalofcriminology.com.

McCaslin, M., and Good, T. (1992). Complaint cognition: The misalliance of management and instructional goals in current school reform. *Educational Researcher 40*(3), 41–50.

McNeely, C. A., Nonnemaker, J. M., and Blum, R. W. (2002). Promoting school connectedness: Evidence from the national longitudinal student of adolescent health. *Journal of School Health 72*, 138–146.

McPartland, J., Jordan, W., Legters, N., and Balfanz, R. (1997). Finding safety in small numbers. *Educational Leadership 55*(2), 14–17.

Mendez, L. M. R. (2003). Predictors of suspension and negative school outcomes: A longitudinal investigation. In J. Wald and D. J. Losen (eds.), *New Directions for Youth Development: Deconstructing the School-to-Prison Pipeline* (pp. 91–120). San Francisco: Jossey-Bass.

Osher, D., Sandler, S., and Nelson, C. (2001, Winter). The best approach to safety is to fix schools and support children and staff. *New Directions in Youth Development 92*, 127–154.

Patterson, V., Roehrig, H., and Luff, J. A. (2003). Running the treadmill: Explorations of beginning high school science teacher turnover in Arizona. *High School Journal 86*(4), 14.

Public Agenda. (2004, May). Teaching interrupted. Retrieved July 26, 2005, from www.publicagenda.org.

Raywid, M.A. (1994). Alternative schools: The state of the art. *Educational Leadership, 52*(1), 26–31.

Resnick, M., Bearman, P., Blum, R., Bauman, K., Harris, J., Tabor, J., Beuhring, T., Sieving, R., Shew, M., Ireland, M., Bearinger, L., and Udry, R. (1997). Protecting adolescents from harm: Findings from the national longitudinal study on adolescent health. *Journal of American Medical Association 278*, 823–832.

U.S. Department of Education, National Center of Educational Statistics. (2005). Indicators of School Crime and Safety. Retrieved July 10, 2005, from nces.ed.gov/programs/crimeindicators/.

U.S. Department of Justice. (1999). Indicators of school crime and safety. Retrieved July 29, 2003, from www.ojp.gov/bjs/pub/ascii/iscs99.txt.

Verdugo, R. (2005). *Zero Tolerance Policies: A Policy Analysis in Draft.* Washington, DC: National Education Association.

Wang, M. C., Haertel, G. D., and Walberg, H. J. (1993). Toward a knowledge base for school learning. *Review of Educational Research 63*, 249–294.

Resources

Achieving Behaving Caring (ABC) Project, University of Vermont

Alternative Schools: Research on Policy, Practice, and Implications for Youth, University of Minnesota, Minneapolis, ici.umn.edu/alternativeschools

Amazing Discoveries, University of Arizona

American Federation of Teachers, 555 New Jersey Avenue, N.W., Washington, DC 20001, 222.aft.org

Applied Research Center, www.arc.org

Behavior Prevention Program, University of Kansas, Kansas City (Juniper Gardens Children Project)

The Center for the Study and Prevention of Violence, University of Colorado, Boulder

Check and Connect, University of Minnesota, Institute of Community Integration

Classroom Management websites, www.ez2bsaved.com/class_manage.htm

Colorado BLUEPRINTS (Promising Programs, Model Programs criteria), www.cspv.org

Communities That Care Prevention Strategies: A Research Guide to What Works, Catalano & Hawkins, 2003

Community Transition Program, University of Oregon

Conflict Resolution/Peer Mediation Project, University of Florida

Consistency Management and Cooperative Discipline, University of Houston, www.coe.uh.edu/cmcd, Jerome Freiberg, freiberg@mail.uh.edu

Department of Health and Human Services, Youth Violence: A Report of the Surgeon General, www.surgeongeneral.gov/library/youthviolence

Hamilton Fish Institute, www.hamfish.org

Hamilton Fish National Institute on School and Community Violence, www.hfni.gsehd.gwu.edu

Harvard Civil Rights Project, www.civilrightsproject.harvard.edu

Improving the Lives of Children, University of North Carolina, Charlotte

Institute on Community Integration, University of Minnesota, Minneapolis, ici.umn.edu

Journal of School Health, September 2004, allaboutkids.umn.edu

Laulima Lokahi, University Affiliated Program, University of Hawaii

Learning in Deed, W. K. Kellogg Foundation Program, www.learningindeed.com

Linkages to Learning Program, University of Maryland

Mentor/Advisor Project, University of Vermont Center on Disability & Community Inclusion

National Association of School Psychologists, www.naspweb.org

National Education Association, www.nea.org

National Resource Center for Safe Schools, www.safetyzone.org

National School Safety Center, www.nssc1.org

Office of Juvenile Justice and Delinquency Prevention (OJJDP), U.S. Department of Justice and the Development Services Group, Inc., www.dsgonline.com

Ohio School Climate Guidelines, www.ode.state.oh.us/students-families-communities/PDF/Ohio%20School_Climate_Guidelines_9-27-04.pdf

Prevention Strategies That Work: What Administrators Can Do To Promote Positive Student Behavior, cecp.air.org/preventionstrategies

Project SERVE, University of Oregon

Project SUCCESS, University of Miami

School Connectedness and Meaningful Student Participation, www.k12coordinator.org/onlinece/onlineevents/connect/index.htm

Strengthening the Safety Net, www.air.org/cecp/safetynet.htm

Supportive Schools, University of Kansas Center on Research and Learning, www.ku-crl.org

About the Author

Professor Augustina H. Reyes teaches courses in principal preparation, school finance, and education law at the University of Houston, where she also directs an urban principal preparation program. In 1999, she received a three-year planning grant from the Sid W. Richardson Foundation of Texas and a follow-up grant from Title III of the U.S. Department of Education. The grants provided funding to complete a study on the preparation of urban school principals using an interdisciplinary, principal-preparation curriculum model in collaboration with the Bauer College of Business and the College of Liberal Arts and Social Sciences. The collaborative principal preparation model produced a core of urban school practitioners with knowledge and skills in management, second language learning, and conditions of low-income families and environments.

Reyes is a former associate professor in the Texas A&M Department of Educational Administration and the TAMU Principal's Center, where she served as the director of the Texas A&M Principal's Institute. As associate director of the TAMU Principal's Institute, Reyes taught courses in principalship, urban education, and school law. She was also a visiting professor at the University of Iowa.

Reyes's career as an educator started in a school in Houston's ship channel area, where her first teaching assignment was a first-grade class with thirty-two students who were repeating the first grade. Her background in Maria Montessori methods earned her the teacher-of-the-year award for her school. "The use of Montessori methods formed and reinforced literacy concepts in the minds of low-income and immigrant students." As a central office administrator, Reyes's work with low-income and ESL students continued. She directed the Houston Independent School District Bilingual Programs for approximately 32,000 students.

Reyes acquired policymaking skills as a trustee for both the Houston Independent School District and Houston Community College. She was on the Houston ISD board of trustees for ten years, serving as president (for two terms), vice president, and secretary. She also served as vice president and secretary for the Houston Community College.

Reyes has published several journal articles, book chapters, and other publications. In 1998, *The Journal of Gender, Race, and Justice, A Journal of the University of Iowa College of Law* published "School Finance, Bilingual Education, and Free Speech." In 2003, "Does Money Make a Difference for Hispanic Students in Urban Schools?" was published in *Education and Urban Society*. In 2001, the *Fordham University School of Law Urban Law Journal* published "Alternative Education: The Criminalization of Student Behavior." Reyes's study, "Criminalization of Student Discipline" was presented in May 2003 at the Harvard Civil Rights Project Conference at the Harvard Graduate School of Education. In 2004, Reyes published "School Finance: Raising Questions for Urban Schools" (with Gloria Rodriguez) in *Education and Urban Society*. A study conducted for the Texas school finance case, *West Orange-Cove Consolidated ISD, et al. v. Shirley Neeley, Texas Commissioner of Education, et al.*, was published in the *Journal of Education Finance* in spring 2006. She also testified as an expert witness in this case.

Four outstanding authors wrote two of the seven chapters in this book. M. Karega Rausch is a research associate with the Indiana Initiative for Equity and Opportunity at the Center for Evaluation and Education Policy at Indiana University, Bloomington. His research interests include issues pertaining to educational equity, specifically minority disproportionality in school discipline and special education. His most recent publications have examined school disciplinary systems including use of zero tolerance school discipline, the extent of usage and the outcomes associated with school disciplinary options, and explored school leaders' use of preventative alternatives to student removal.

Russell J. Skiba is the director of the Indiana Initiative for Equity and Opportunity at the Center for Evaluation and Education Policy and professor of Learning, Development, and Psychological Sciences at Indiana University. He has worked with schools across the country in the management of disruptive behavior, school discipline, and school violence and has published in the areas of school violence, zero tolerance, and equity in education. He is currently a member of the American Psychological Association's Task Force on Zero Tolerance, has testified before both Houses of Congress on issues of school discipline and school violence and was awarded the Push for Excellence Award by the Rainbow Coalition/Operation PUSH for his work on African American disproportionality in school suspension.

Ronnie Casella is associate professor of educational foundations and secondary education at Central Connecticut State University. He is the author of several books, including *Being Down: Challenging Violence in Urban Schools* and *At Zero Tolerance: Punishment, Prevention, and School Violence*. He has also published articles in *Urban Review, International Journal of Qualitative Studies in Education, Qualitative Inquiry, Teachers College Record,* and *Anthropology and Education Quarterly*.

Johanna Wald is a freelance writer and former senior development/policy analyst at the Civil Rights Project at Harvard University. She served as coprincipal investigator on a research project documenting the perspectives and attitudes of teachers on school discipline and as coauthor of a series of reports and articles related to the school-to-prison pipeline and school dropouts. She helped to write the first national report documenting racial disparities in the application of school discipline (*Opportunities Suspended*, 2000) and to organize a national summit on zero tolerance. She served as the lead editor for a journal entitled *Deconstructing the School-to-Prison Pipeline* (2004). Her articles, reports, and op-eds on these issues have appeared in salon.com, *The Boston Globe, The Nation, School Board Association Newsletter, Boston Law Journal,* and *Center for American Progress*.